As You Wish, Mother

H. Ramlath

FanatiXx Publication
ISO 9001:2015 CERTIFIED

FanatiXx Publication
AM/56, Basanti Colony, Rourkela 769012, Odisha
ISO 9001:2015 CERTIFIED
Website: *www.fanatixxpublication.com*

© **Copyright, 2023, H. Ramlath**

All rights reserved. No part of this book may be reproduced, stored in a retrieval system, or transmitted, in any form by any means, electronic, mechanical, magnetic, optical, chemical, manual, photocopying, recording or otherwise, without prior written consent of the author.

"As You Wish, Mother"
By: H. Ramlath
ISBN: 978-93-5452-592-6
1st Edition
Cover Design: Noorleen Kaur Bhatia
Price: 220.00 INR
Printed and Typeset by: BooksClub.in

The opinions/ contents expressed in this book are solely of the author and do not represent the opinions/ stands/ thoughts of FanatiXx.

Disclaimer

This is a work of fiction. Names, characters, places, and incidents are either the product of author's imagination or have been used illustratively and any resemblance to any person, living or dead, events or locales is entirely coincidental.

H. Ramlath asserts all rights to be identified as the author of this work.

To my Mother...

About the Author

Ramlath is an aspiring debut writer. 'As you wish, Mother' is her debut work. Her love for books made her study literature. She loves to dwell in the wild imaginary world where she can let her dreams fly. Her journey as a writer just started, and she has a long way to go. She knows hard work never fails and that each step counts. Her writings point out typical family-oriented situations and concentrate on daily life. Her writing style is simple and focuses on daily life.

Acknowledgment

This book wouldn't be possible without these people in my life. Each one of them inspired me in various ways.

First of all, I have to thank the universe which put me into situations that made me who I am today.

My college, the safest place in the world, where I let my fantasies fly. This is the place where I was given opportunities to explore myself.

My teachers helped me to enhance myself. I thank you for being patient with me and letting me know my potential.

My friends, Kirupa, Isvarya, and Vidyamani. Thank you for reading my work patiently and giving your honest reviews. Thank you for reading my work millions of times.

I thank Ripal and Authors gully for their constant support and guidance to find a publisher.

I thank FanatiXx publishers and their team for being with me throughout this journey. I thank Saizal for being patient while editing and for the support.

As You Wish, Mother

1

It is midnight. Everyone is asleep except for one. Lumra gets out of her bed after making sure that her brother is sleeping, and she moves to her parent's room. She checks on her parents, they are deep into sleep. She closes the door quietly. Lumra wore her favorite floral-designed red nightdress; she tied her hair in a messy bun and walked stealthily to her study room, groping in the dark. Without wasting time, she quickly takes a bounded book on the table and placesit under a heap of notes. She opens it and pens down her thoughts. A few minutes later, she carefully wraps it in a leather cloth and places it exactly from where she took it. No one in her family knew about this diary or her thoughts and plans for her life. She doesn't want to think beyond this. All that she wants now is to be free and happy. She switched off the lamp and spread herself all over the bed, smiling… Suddenly, *what about tomorrow?* This thought made her think about what she wrote in her diary. She slowly led her thoughts to the moment she spoke with her friend….

Dear Pinky,

I Love you so much. Being my best friend (you must already know by now,) only you know who I am and my true self, which is hidden from everyone else's eyes. Thank you so much, Pinky, for being there for me always, you may be seen as a lifeless note by others, but only I know what will happen if you are not there for me. Ok, I'll come to the point. You know, tomorrow is going to be an amazing day because college is reopening....Woohoo!!!!! I felt so bored during this summer vacation, I don't know why people are very fond of this vacation, but I don't like it. I just want to be in college and read as many books as possible, and live in a world where no one is going to trouble me. Anyway, I have a piece of good news for you. Do you remember the marriage proposal which came for me? I think that proposal is no more in consideration. I am not sure about it, but I think it is over. I am very afraid of these proposals. I don't know why people can't understand the fact that first, a girl should stand on her own to create her own identity. Is it necessary to get married at this age? Like, I am just twenty for now, so why this early?

Somehow I escaped this time, but the next time 'Allah'.... help me.

Ok, Pinky, Good night; I need to wake up early tomorrow, so see you later.

Love you,
Lumra

Lumra is a twenty-year-old girl, good-looking and kind-hearted, ambitious and determined with lots of passion. She has brown eyes and a fair complexion, but she looks absurd in some people's eyes due to her behavior. She is crazyfor literary characters, while girls of her age keep on falling in love with film characters. She loves writers and their works, while others droolover celebrities and their lifestyles; she never cares about these things. She always wants to be simple in her way of dressing and looks. This makes her mother aggressive because she wants her daughter to look as beautiful as other girls, "the voice of a typical Indian Mother."

If one peeps into her heart but cannot, one may find her to be a girl who always chooses to keep everyone happy around her and always makes sure that no one gets hurt. She is secretive, sensitive, and intelligent yet has a childlike innocent nature. She lives in Vellore, a city in Tamil Nadu, India. Vellore is known for its scorching heat and lined-up stores and shops. Vellore is a paradise for all sellers. Here, Lumra belongs to a middle-class family, having only the basic expectations in their life. She seems to be a fish out of the tank. She wants to touch the stars while her family is content to enjoy their beauty from afar. She is the eldest daughter; her brother is studying in the tenth standard. Both are like Tom and Jerry, they fight a lot, yet they can't live apart. Jokes of Suhail and the smile of Lumra fill the home most often.

With a smile on her face, she was thinking about her life.

She looked for her phone here and there, set the alarm for 7 am, and kept it aside. Her mind was occupied with curiosity for the following day. Happiness has knocked on her door after a long time; she goes to bed with a light heart and sleeps peacefully.

"I don't know what we are going to do with her?" Zainab moans to her husband in a feeble voice.

"Why? Why are you suddenly saying all this?" Manzoor asks with a quizzical look.

"You know... I like that family, but I don't think their character will be to our daughter's liking. Whenever I think about her, my headaches. What will she do if we are not with her? She is twenty, but she still behaves like a child."

"Zainab, don't worry. She will change; give her some time."

"What time! She is twenty. Sooner or later, she has to get married."

"You already know that she has this behaviour you upset about it now?"

"Now! She becomes sad whenever there is a proposal and starts sobbing as if we have slapped her. She thinks that we are unaware of this drama. Before ,it was fine, as she was a little girl, but now she is twenty and should prepare for marriage. She can't stay here with us always, right? And I don't know how long we will live in this world. Before we die, I want to ensure that my daughter lives happily."

"Don't worry about this; trust Allah! Believe him, and he will take care of our daughter. Time will change everything; now, go to sleep. Tomorrow we have to wake up early and work or else we won't be able to afford our children's needs and other things. Leave all these thoughts aside and sleep now."

"Yes. I have to settle many things tomorrow."

Zainab is Lumra's mother; she is forty-seven years old. Her family is her only world. She works hard even at this age, always thinking about her children's future. She can sacrifice anything for them. She often couldn't even get up from bed, but she did, thinking about her children's future. Her legs pain a lot after standing in her shop for the whole day. She ceaselessly ensures that her children receive the best of everything.

Lumra's father, Manzoor, is fifty years old. He has faced many troubles in his life, so he doesn't want his children to face the same. He pushes himself to work more, so their children can enjoy their childhood and be happy.

Zainab and Manzoor drifted into a deep sleep, thinking about their children.

Parents are incredible beings who sacrifice their lives to give a good life to their children. But, sometimes, in their efforts they forget that their children, too have their priorities in life.

2

"Wake up,Lumra, it's time to pray. And don't you remember you have to get ready for College? Did you forget that you have College?" Zainab calls out. But Lumra did not stir up.
"You are a girl, Lumra. You cannot sleep till late once you get married. If you do, what will your in-laws say about us and our upbringing." Zainab started yelling.

Lumra wakes up from her bed; she doesn't want this topic to continue as she knows that this marriage conversation will prolong, and she doesn't want that to happen. She wants to go to college in a happy mood. She sighs and mumbles to her mother that she woke up and walked straight to refresh. She prays her early morning prayer, then she enters the kitchen to cook breakfast for her whole family and lunch for her brother, who has school till the evening. Since her parents go to their shop early in the morning, Lumra cooks most of the time.

"Suhail, wake up! It's already late, dad will come at any time from the market, so before that you should get ready. Wake up, you idiot, it's already time; I can't be late to college on the first day itself; get up!" Lumra shouts at Suhail and pulls him out of bed.

Suhail slowly wakes up, and he goes to get ready. Lumra has already kept all his things ready on the table because she knows he will search for everything only at the last moment.

Suhail pranks Lumra all the time, but he is so polite to others and is a class topper. Lumra's Parents never show any partiality to their children. They give equal importance to both. Whoever commits a mistake gets punished. They never give special attention to Suhail because of his gender, which is considered superior in our society. He was raised knowing this. So, Suhail has never shown any anthropocentric attitude towards her.

Manzoor comes home from the market. Both Lumra and Suhail are ready. Manzoor always drops them in their respective college and school. Lumra is very excited about this day. She loves to be in her college more than any other place; sometimes, she even loves to stay in college than be at home. They go to college in his two-wheeler. Manzoor drops Lumra at the entrance of her college. She tells Manzoor that she will call him as soon as the college gets over.

Lumra studies at Praesidium College, which is one of the best women's colleges in her place. Her college is of many blocks; her class is in the Arts block, which is an old block. It is known for its gigantic look. There are three-way staircases; two are in the corners and one in the center. Lumra walks through the right-side staircase. She feels very happy to be back and is excited to meet her friends. She climbs the stairs very fast and enters the classroom, not many students are in the classroom. She says 'Hi' to everyone and removes her burkha.

The college bell rings, and students start entering the classroom. But Lumra waits for some special ones to enter. She starts laughing at the two girls, breathless, trying to outdo each other, and barge into the classroom.

Grace and Shafiya are Lumra's close and only friends.

"How do you both manage to get late always? You both are *Late Lateef*." Lumra laughs.

"The thing is, we both are not much punctual as you, Ms. Perfect." Grace hugs Lumra and giggles.

"This morning was hectic, Lumra. First, I need to do all the work at home, and secondly, I missed a bus today. The next bus came after 30 minutes. Now tell me, how can I reach on time?" Shafiyasaid in a single breath.

"Ok…Ok….Leave it,Shafiya."

Before Grace or Shafiya could say anything, Lumra immediately said, "Ma'am is coming, let's take our places fast."

Grace is the last bencher, although not among those who used to mock teachers, make fun of others or just attend college to enjoy; she justloves sitting there. Shafiya and Lumra are bench partners too.

"Good Morning Ma'am." The class greeted Selvi Ma'am."

It's a routine in Praesidum College to begin the first lecture by taking God's name. So Selvi ma'am asked everyone to pray.

"It's good to see you all today. I guess, no one is absent today. Hope you enjoyed your summer holidays very much and now you have come to college without any interest, is it?" Selvi ma'am asks slyly. But the whole class denies it and tells her that they are very much interested to come to College.

"If that is true then I am happy." Says Selvi Ma'am while flipping the pages of her register in which she probably writes all the important updates and notices. After a pause, she says, "Girls, there is an announcement, I thought of informing you first so that you can start preparing a little earlier. Our college is going to conduct an international conference, UG final-year students can participate. For the conference you should submit an article, I know that you girls are not yet familiar with the works cited and documentation, but I will brief you regarding those. I want you to take part in it and present papers, as it will add additional weight to your degree. For an article, you should select one literary work and analyze it properly. For this, you need to pay only Four hundred rupees; this offer is only for students. The word limit is 2000 I guess….I will provide the brochure to your class representative. She will distribute it to you. Take this opportunity, you might not get one again.

We will leave this matter for a while, now I'll give you an outline of what I am going to teach this semester. At the end of the hour, those who are interested give me your names."

Then she started her lessons. The students in the class were stunned by her teaching and listened keenly.

Lumra admires Selvi ma'am and her teaching more than the other students. For Lumra she is her idol. Because when Lumra was in her first year, she had to give a speech on her favourite author, but she couldn't because of fear. That incident was her transforming moment.

"Hi. Girls, I am Lumra….." *Lumra! don't….don't do this….if you stutter in front of the class they will laugh at you…Allah, please help me….*

"I am going to talk about my favourite author….my fav…ourite….author….is" clears her throat, which is dry, takes a deep breath, all over her body shivers and she starts to perspire a lot.

"My favourite author is……." She feels someone's hand around her.

Selvi ma'am puts her hand around Lumra's shoulder and tells everyone in the class that she scored well in her exams. She was able to achieve this even though her medium of instruction at school was different.

Then she tells in her ear, "You did great, don't worry go….. sit at your place and drink some water. Relax!"

As You Wish, Mother

This chant nurtured and encouraged her to speak in English frequently and fluently. From that day onwards, she tried hard to overcome her fears. She took up every single chance on her way to speak in front of the class. Her frequent practice made her one of the good speakers in her class, but still, she tries to improve herself.

Selvi Ma'am finished introducing her portions.
"Now tell me girls, who all are interested in this international conference?"

No one in the class raised their hands. Lumra wants to raise her hand but she couldn't, something restrained her from raising her hand.

Should I raise my hand or not? What if I fail? It would be great if I publish my work at an international conference but even class toppers didn't raise their hands what can I do then? Oh my! What do I do now? Her thoughts were interrupted by Selvi ma'am.

"Girls, you never value the importance of opportunities, you don't know how many students of your age desperately wait for this kind of occasion. You will never get a chance like this often. You should always be prepared to claim such opportunities which

lurk right under your nose. 'Once you lose, you lose it forever.' So, think about it, I can only show you the way but it's you who decide to take this path." In a serious tone, she advises her students as she does not want them to lose this golden opportunity.
"Now tell me who wants to join, if no one is interested I'll leave as I have another class to teach."

Agalya, their Class representative gave her name, and immediately a few hands shot up. I think it's true that if you want to break through and step forward you need someone to push you. We are always afraid to take a new path. Even Lumra needs a push, I think she got it, let us see what she chooses. To sit back or raise her hand?

Lumra understands that she cannot remain passive forever, so she raises her hand, at last.
God, please help me. Give your strength to my heart and hands. I have raised my hand, so lead me in a good way till the end. Allah, please.

Her hands nervously shook as they stood in the air amidst other hands. The cool breeze gave strength to her and it seemed promising.
She will do her best, she gained confidence in herself, and even Grace and Shafiya gave their names.

The teacher asks a few girls what they are planning to write then she turns to Lumra.

"Lumra, do you want to present a paper?"

"Yes ma'am, I want to."

"That's good. What genre are you planning to do?"

"Ma'am, I am thinking of children's literature. Can I do my presentation on children's fiction ma'am?"

"Yes, you can."

The bell rings. Selvi ma'am leaves for the next class. The rest of the day teachers came, they discussed their syllabus, about the student's vacations, and their class ended. Finally, it's time to go home but Lumra, Grace, and Shafiya remain for a while in the classroom.

"We gave our names but do you have any idea about what has to be done?" Shafiya asks.

"I don't have any idea; do you have anything, Grace?" Lumra asks.

Heyyy... I thought you already had an idea because you told ma'am about the genre you are going to work on."

"Do you think only with that I can complete my article? You brilliant!"

"Oh! Yes, I get it, you're brilliant... Anyway, can we go to the library today?" Asks Grace.

"Yes, we can." Says Lumra.

"What about you Shafiya?"

"Sorry, Grace. I can't because I didn't inform my father and I have some work at home."

"Oh, that's ok. Take care."

Then the three emerged from their classroom, Shafiya wears her burkha and they come down the center staircase.

"What about the proposal which came to you Lumra?" Shafiya asked.

"I think it's dropped. You know, I am really happy about it. For this only I prayed to Allah, I asked him that it should somehow be stopped. Thank you, Allah! You helped me this time." She replies happily.

"Lumra, kindly don't mistake me, one can't pray like this, this is not at all good," Shafiya said in a worried manner.

"I know, Shafiya. Don't worry I never prayed like I should not get married at all, I just prayed to Allah that I just need some time. This is my life, Shafiya, I've never experienced my life to its fullest, never explored those things which I always wanted and I don't believe that this is the right age for me to get married. You know, I want to become a popular person. Even after my death, I want this world to remember my name. I don't want to die as "she was just one among the many in this world", I want to be someone who leaves behind some legacy in this world."

She stops to catch her breath and says, "Why is no one ready to understand marriage from my viewpoint? Ok, leave it, we have reached the library. Bye, Shafiya. Travel safely and sorry if I hurt you."

"No, don't be sorry. You did not hurt me. It's just that I am worried about you. Anyways, take care girls. See you tomorrow."

It was a tiring day for both Zainab and Manzoor. From morning customers were continuously coming to their shop, so they didn't have time to take rest. Today, the work was too much so Zainab did not get a chance to go home to prepare lunch.

It was 2 in the afternoon, Manzoor generally closes his shop from 2 pm to 4 pm daily, so that he could get some rest.

As soon as the couple entered the house, Zainab started cooking and Manzoor left to masque for Namaz. Later, Zainab sets everything on the dining table. Manzoor entered the house telling 'Assalamualaikum', Zainab greets him back. They sit together at the dining table and start eating. At that moment Manzoor's phone starts ringing. He gets up to answer his phone.

"What? When did this happen? How?" He asks shockingly.

"We can't do anything, all these incidents are pre-

written we can't change. We should accept his actions. In sha Allah, I'll try to come."
Then he hangs the phone. But, his face looks very pale. Zainab didn't know what happened and she panics looking at his face.

"What happened? Why are you looking so sad? Did something happen?" Zainab asks with concern.

"Do you remember Wasim Bhai?" Manzoor asks.

"Yes, I know. Sometimes he comes to our shop to visit you. You also told me that he has two daughters, the elder one looks like our Lumra. What happened to him?"

"He is no more."

Zainab couldn't digest what she heard, she stood shocked.

"What? When did it happen?"

"Even I don't know. They said that he had a heart attack."

"Oh, Allah should take care of him and his family." Replies Zainab.

"What about his daughters, are they married?" Zainab asks.

"No, they are not. He was in search of a groom for the elder one, but before anything could happen he lost his life.

Manzoor takes a deep breath. They began to eat silently. This conversation became more personal to Zainab because her thoughts raced to Lumra. "What will happen to Lumra when she dies?" This thought weighed her heart down and bothered her immensely, but she didn't show it out or hint it to Manzoor.

For a mother, it is really difficult to even imagine her life without her daughter. Parents after hearing about such unfortunate incidents start to worry about their children's life, especially when one of them is a girl.

Zainab is going through the same series of thoughts. Now she is getting more worried about the apple of her eye-Lumra.

3

Lumra and Grace enter the library which is behind Art's block. This library is one of the oldest buildings in their college, but it contains the whole magnanimity of it. Inside the library, they have all types of books from science to Arts, History, Psychology, and Fiction. They have thousands and thousands of books for each department. Whenever Lumra enters the library she feels some strange connection with books. For Lumra, the fiction section is the dearest one. She loves to read a lot and books alone can make her happy. She even wrote a few short stories and poems but never showed them to anyone, as she thought they will laugh at them. Her stories always have her personal touch, which she feels will bore others.

On entering the library Lumra and Grace greet the librarian, Maria. The librarian is one of the kindest persons Lumra has ever come across. She too likes Lumra very much and always suggests interesting

books and the latest arrivals to her. She smiles at Lumra when she hears them.
"Ma'am, I want keys to the reference section", asks Lumra.

"Why do you want those?" Asks Maria.

"Ma'am we are going to do a paper presentation at an international conference. We need some journals and articles for references", explains Grace.

"Ok, before going to the reference section, register your information in this register note", says the librarian.

She hands over the keys to Lumra. Both of them recorded their information and head toward the reference section.
The reference section room is a very quiet place, only the research scholars and teachers visit this section. Lumra enters the room and opens the cupboard using the key given by the librarian. The cupboard was filled with keys of the bureaus of the reference section. Suddenly she heard a shriek then a whisper and its echoes.

"Oh my! This room is so dark and scary what will happen if someone comes behind that cupboard and shows the knife to us…" Lumra turns around it was Grace pranking, which is her typical hobby. Grace starts to act as if she is afraid and hides behind one of the bureaus. Lumra starts to giggle after looking at the actions of the drama queen.

"Shut up, Grace. What are you doing?" Asks Lumra smiling slyly, acting cool.
"What if a ghost comes behind you, If it comes I am going to leave it with you and I will run", Grace didn't finish her drama still.

"If a ghost comes I will kick that ghost and tell the ghost that I am already a GHOST'S friend." She replies pointing at Grace.

"OH FUNNY. I am not a ghost. Do I look like one? Mmmm…. Maybe I do. Then look I am floating…..blah!!! blah!!!" (She mimics Dracula's cry)

"Yes, you are the GHOST." Lumra mocks Grace. Then she points behind Grace, and both freeze. Then they start to laugh, "if someone comes to the reference

section now, they will think that we are mad and they will book two seats in a mental asylum, and then we need to do our presentation there only." Says Lumra.
"Hahaha…Ok…Let us start to search materials for our presentation", says Grace.

Lumra opens the cupboard and searchedthe English Department section keys and takes it. They fish for the racks containing projects, journals, and articles. They take some notes and acted like English scholars writing and made fun of each other.
The time flies and Grace reminds Lumra that it's almost 3 pm.
"What? 3'o clock? I didn't even inform my parents that I will be late. Let's go, we will finish this later." Says Lumra.
"Fine by me."

Then they closed all cupboards and locked the room. They took the reference section keys to hand them over to the librarian. Lumra wears her burkha and they start walking to their bus stop. They get into a bus and reach their stop. Both Lumra and Grace love to talk while they walk to their home, they talk about many things. Lumra always talks to Grace in English, to improve her

As You Wish, Mother

vocabulary and fluency. Today they are conversing about their first-ever paper presentation.

"Can we visit the library tomorrow also? We need to take some more references and can you inform this to Shafiya?" Asks Lumra.

"Ok, we will go to the library tomorrow and I will surely inform her."

"Then bring lunch tomorrow."

"Ok, Lumi. I will."

They reach Grace's house. Lumra starts to walk alone, she recalls the happening of the day, it has been a magical day for her. She feels happy to know how much she has improved herself, and this confidence gives her the energy to achieve anything. She desperately wants to complete her presentation successfully. She believes this platform will help her to move on with her life and she will attain what she wants. She reaches her home. She is now super excited to tell her mother how her daughter for the first time raised her hand to prove herself.

As You Wish, Mother

"Ma, I am home."

"Why so late?" Asks Zainab.

"Sorry Ma, I went to the library and I forgot to call you." Replies Lumra and she continue with excitement, "Ma, I have something to tell you."

"First, go, freshen up and do some household chores. I am going to open shop." Says Zainab.

Lumra got a little disappointment but she understands her mother. So, she prepares tea for her parents and starts cleaning the kitchen.

Around 8'o clock Zainab is in the store looking after her customers. Lumra comes to the shop in excitement she jumped a little and tells, "Ma, today Selvi Ma'am informed all of usof something important."

"How many times do I need to tell you to stand properly, don't jump? Now you are grown up and not a child anymore." Scolds Zainab. Lumra was silent and stood still there then Zainab asks, "why did you come here?"

"Ma, in our college they are going to conduct an international seminar, that means many people will come from abroad, so ma'am wants some people from our class should participate and Selvi ma'am selected some of us, even I am included in that, She tells her mother." (She lied to her mother because she feels if she tells the truth she will not allow her, other than this she never lied to her mother). "For that, we have to pay just Four hundred rupees." Says Lumra.

"When do you have to pay that amount?"

"I don't know Ma, Ma'am just told this information only; I'll ask her about it tomorrow." Replies Lumra.

By this time all her excitement vanished and her voice became weary.

"Did you finish all the work?" Asks Zainab.

"Yes, Ma, what do I need to cook for dinner?"

"Cook Chapati and sambhar."

"Ok, Ma."

She goes to her home and starts cooking. In between, she plans within herself what she is going to do in her presentation. She just doesn't want to lose any opportunities which come her way. She is very eager to do something that will change her life.

After finishing her dinner, she cleans the kitchen and enters her room. She started to write her ideas that were running in her mind while she was cooking. Then something sparked. So she asks her brother, "Hey Suhail, what you will do if I became popular?" Suddenly Suhail bursts into laughter and says, "You…You are becoming popular, so funny." It hurts Lumra but she just wants to ask her brother that could she be popular, someday.

"Do you think you can be popular suddenly? Don't evoke laughter to me." Then he goes to sleep. But, Lumra couldn't. Her brother's laugh echoed in her mind and she could listen to it. She goes to her study room.

Dear Pinky,

You know, today is one of those days where I cried in happiness and sadness. I don't know whether I should rejoice in happiness or sit alone and think about the disappointment. I don't want you to get confused. So wait, I'll tell you what happened today. You know for the first time in the past three years I raised my hand in my class that too for an international conference. Yes, I am going to present a paper. I was surprised by my action even Selvi ma'am was amazed. She was very proud of me. For the first time, I trust myself and raised my hands. This made my day in college. It was contrary at home, I came home very excited because I just want to tell mom that her daughter for the first time broke all her fears and believed in herself completely, and going to participate in the international conference. But all I received was disappointment. She scolded me for jumping in excitement and asked me whether I grew up or not. I just jumped, nothing else. Is a girl even prohibited to jump in joy on this earth? I don't know, Pinky. Added to that my brother, I just asked him what he will do if I became popular and all that he did was laugh at me and made fun of me. Do you too think similarly, Pinky? I am very offended.

I am not able to enjoy what I did today. I think I can't enjoy anything that could make me happy. I don't know.

While writing this tears filled her eyes, she tries to control them, but, all that she helds from evening gushed out from her eyes and at last, she let them dry

I am thankful to you Pinky because without you I would have burst out long before, but you made me stable. Love you Pinky.

With love,
Lumra.

***

Zainab looks worried. Manzoor asks her, "Zainab what happened? Why are you looking so worried?"

"I am thinking about our daughter, she still behaves like a child. She is a grown-up and soon she will get married to someone. If she still behaves like this, what will happen to her? Life not always offers you a bed of roses, along with it comes the thorns too. She will face many trials in one way or other, which might break her into tiny pieces. She needs to become strong and smart now. She has to understand that straight trees are cut first. I am not saying that she could not handle problems, but she believes that apart from a few, every other person on this beautiful earth is genuine. We will not be always there to hold her hand and guide her through the path. This makes me worried, Manzoor."

"Our child is so pure and we never let her out that's why she is not aware of anything. We should give her a chance, only then she will learn. Everything has a right time, so don't worry about her, just pray to Allah, he will take care of everything."
Then both of them go to sleep.

Even though both mother and daughter love each other abundantly, they fail to understand each other's feelings.
Do you think it will change in the future? Hope for the best.

4

"Hey, how are you Azeema?" Asked Zainab,

"I am fine. Why didn't you come to my daughter's wedding, only Manzoor came?"

"I was not well and you know about my situation, someone should take care of the store, or else it will be hard to manage our daily allowance, nowadays it's very tough to hold customers also."

Azeema was Zainab's neighbor and a good friend. She knows how much Zainab and Manzoor work hard to fulfill their primary and secondary needs.

"Yes, that is true. How are you now? Feeling better?"

"Yes, I am ok now. How was your daughter's marriage? How is she now? Is everything fine in her in-law's house?"

"Marriage was great, I didn't expect such before, a crowd, and everyone was talking about the grand decoration and food only. Even her In-laws and relatives were happy. I was worried about my girl but now, I am very happy. All my worries have now vanished. She is very happy there and I advised her to adjust with the family in all situations because the acceptance of a girl only stabilizes the family."

For ages, it has always been women who are asked to adjust to whatever the situation is. Our society has shaped us in such a manner that no matter what, single-sex is expected to fit in either by hook or by crook.

Azeema continued, "I wanted to ask you, what happened to the proposal that came for your daughter? Is everything all right?"

"No, I didn't feel they were good for Lumra. So, I canceled it."

"It's ok. Everything happens according to God's plan so, don't worry."

Zainab nods with a fake smile on her face and says, "I am not worried about the proposal, I am just worried about Lumra, whenever we talk about marriage, she becomes very polite and she secludes herself from us, most importantly she starts to cry, I don't know what to do with her."

Azeema senses the worry in her friend's voice so she consoles her, "This is normal. Don't worry she is still a child. Till now she is all pampered. She feels insecure when she thinks about marriage, you proceed with your work, she will be all right when she gets married. We, their parents only know and do what is always good for them. Am I right?"

"Yes, you are. I think this is all my fault, I should have told her all about this before I let her join the college. Now she is telling me that studying is more important, let us see what Allah's plan is."

A satisfying conversation was all Zainab needed. She was pleased with what her friend Azeema said but deep inside, she was still worried about her innocent daughter. Zainab wanted Lumra to get married and settle down with her husband and in-laws, whereas, day by day, Lumra was leaning more toward studies.

"Finally, I finished the fair copy of my Presentation," Lumra shouts in her home at midnight in excitement then suddenly shuts her mouth using her hands. Lumra finishes her paper and she can't believe the outcome. Nearly the whole week she had put her heart and soul into this work. She didn't think of anything other than her paperwork.

The next day at her college she shows her paperwork to her friends and they were surprised.

"Wow! That's great Lumra, show that to me." Grace appreciates her. She gives the paper to her friend. Grace and Shafiya check whether it has any grammatical mistakes, then she returns it to her. They both patted Lumra's back.
Shafiya and Grace were supportive of Lumra. Everyone must have friends like these, who are there for you, in sickness and in health, in happiness and in sadness.

Later Lumra goes to meet Ms.Selvi to submit her paper because first, she will correct it then the selected paper

will be sent for Publication. She enters the department. She sees Ms.Selvi correcting some papers.

"Excuse me, ma'am," and hands over the paper to Ms. Slevi.

"Did you finish?" Ms. Selvi asks her in astonishment.

"Yes, ma'am," Lumra replies very proudly.

"Good Lumra. I think you worked hard on this. I'll check your paper and call you. You know one thing, you are the first one in your class to submit the paper."

"Thank you, ma'am."

Lumra is very happy to be praised by her favourite teacher. She could have danced with happiness if she would have been somewhere else than college.

Lumra went home, she couldn't believe what happened today. She goes to her Mom.

"Ma, today Selvima'am, praised me telling me that I am the first one who submitted the paperwork for the conference, I am very happy, Ma."

"I know my Daughter, she is perfect in everything. When will they publish it?"

"After ma'am corrects my paper she will send it to the journal, and they will publish it. If our teachers like my work they will ask me to present it during the conference. This international conference is supposed to happen at our college. They will select a handful of us only since other college students and staff who are participating are given preference to present their paper at our college."

"Ok, I'll give you the fee, first thing tomorrow, go pay it. Ok?"

"Yes, Ma."

Lumra finished all her work today. She didn't expect that this day would bring this much happiness to her. She eats with her family and then goes to sleep. As usual, she wakes up at midnight to write her diary, but today she doesn't have anything to cry for, she wrote all her happy moments that happened today, and with this satisfaction, she goes to sleep again. She doesn't want to think about any other thing now, she just wants to enjoy this moment.

A little appreciation gave Lumra immense happiness. A positive reception is a must in everyone's life, it gives motivation and spreads positivity.

We don't know whether her happiness is going to last for long or not, but I am happy that she is happy for now. What about you?

5

The international conference is getting near so everyone in the college works consistently for its success. The papers were corrected and sent to publications. Now, it's time to prepare the college for the conference, all sections of the English department were allotted many different works,and all of them were busy with their work. Lumra and her class are taking care of the main hall decorations where the officials and chief guests are going to give seminars.

Lumra gives a deep sigh and whispers, "So from here only they are going to give their seminars."

Her eyes are sparkling like stars while she looks at the stage.

There's something in Lumra's eyes. Her eyes speak more than her words. Her eyes are expressive. When she is happy, one can see it in her eyes, when she is sad, her eyes sing songs of gloominess and when she is excited, her eyes shine like stars in the sky.

"Yes, they are, Miss." Grace heard Lumra whispering.

"One day, I want to be like that, I just wanna climb on stage after having achieved something in my future. I want to come to our college as a successful person and I want to inspire people in the world, just like how many people inspired me to live. I want to leave some mark in this world even after my death."

"You will, one day." Replies Grace.

"Insha Allah."

"Lumra! Wait up, miss. Lumra please can I have your autograph……..LumraMaaaddddaaam." Grace acts as if she is her fan and pretends as if she is begging for her autograph.

"Ok, ok. Don't worry, I'll give you my autograph." Lumra too pretends as if she is signing in Grace's hand.

"Ok, enough, for now, I want to ask you something, Lumra," asks Grace.

Lumra laughs a little and nods.
"Who are all selected in UG for Paper Presentation? Because on that day Selvima'am told that due to many

participants, only a few UG students will be selected for presentation."

"Even I was thinking about that." Replies Shafiya entering in the middle of the conversation.

"Somehow Grace will be selected I think." Says Shafiya.

"I don't think so," Grace says.

"Don't act, madam." Lumra laughs and Grace continues, "I believe Lumra will be selected for the paper presentation."

"Don't prank me." Her mouth says so but her heart murmurs 'Insha Allah' because she too wants to present, she too wants to experience it, but she is not sure whether she is going to be selected. She knows there are many bright students in her class. So, she thinks that she will not have much chance.
"I will never prank you in these things, really your work is awesome," Grace tells her smiling yet in a serious tone. "All the best and Congrats ma'am." This gives energy to Lumra but she doesn't show that to anyone.

"Insha Allah. Let us see."

After finishing all their work the students went to their classrooms. Then, their class representative Agalya tells the students to be quiet as Selvima'am entered their classroom. As usual, Selvi ma'am looks vibrant and elegant in her saree.

"Grace, Shafiya, Agalya, Nimmy, and Lumra stand up." Ms.Selvi points out to five people.

When Selvi ma'am utters her name Lumra looks confused, she couldn't understand what is happening then slowly she composes herself(she couldn't get why Selvi ma'am called her, and that too along with these bright students). She stands up slowly.

"Girls you are all selected to present your paper. So, prepare yourself and if you want some help ask me. I am here to help you. Now, all of you be quiet, we have a meeting today in the department, so I am going. Girls come and meet me after the bell (pointing to Lumra and others)." She tells them and goes. Lumra couldn't believe what happened just now, for the first time in her life she'd been recognized by someone, and that someone is none other than her idol. She is selected along with those bright students who inspired her at the beginning of college.

"Is that real?" Lumra asks herself in excitement.

Grace and Shafiya come to her. They shake her up.

"Congrats Lumra."

"WHAT? Oh, sorry girls, I am bewildered now. Spare me for a moment." Lumra is still in shock.

After a couple of minutes, Lumra hugs her friends and says, "We did it."

"I already told you that you will be selected. Look you are selected now." Says Grace

"Thank you, Grace." Lumra replies with happiness.

***

"What? Ok. I'll discuss it with him and then let you know." Zainab switched off her phone and turned towards Manzoor.

As You Wish, Mother

"What is it?" Manzoor asks Zainab.

"She is my distant relative. She told me that she knows one boy in Chennai and she suggested his name for our Lumra."

"Where does he work? What is his name?" Manzoor asks her.

"He is a Software Engineer working in Chennai. His name is Muthahar. He is thirty."

Manzoor is in deep thought, Zainab understands what is running in his mind, so she tells him, "Are you thinking about his age, even I am thinking about the same because our daughter is just twenty and he is thirty. But we need to think about other things too. He is well educated he will take care of our child better, I am not saying that we will get her married to him; we can't make any hasty move, we will think first, then make a decision. What is your opinion?"

"OK, we will think and decide. I think our daughter will come in any time soon. So, we will talk about it later." Says Manzoor.

Lumra enters her home. Then she eats and takes some rest. She wants to tell her mother that she got selected for the paper presentation. But, she is not in a good mood now, she has overheard the conversation between her parents. Even though she believed her parents will think about it a lot, she feels hurt and she is very sad about it. Later, she controls her emotions and prays to Allah, and then starts her work. she plans to inform about her presentation at dinner time.

While eating dinner she tells her parents that her paper got selected for presentation. She informs them that it is a great opportunity for her. Both of her parents were proud of their daughter.

Lumra enters her room after finishing writing her diary (while writing she goes into deep sorrow and cries). Even though she believes her mother, she is afraid of only one thing that is what if all her dreams get shattered into pieces? Will she live happily afterward? She wants to make her parents proud, will it happen? She doesn't want to lose this chance of presenting a paper at the conference, she wants to prove who she is to her parents. She wants to make her parents realize that education is important and she loves to study. For this, she needs to present her paper successfully. She starts to prepare for her seminar which is going to take part in college the next day. After some time she goes to sleep, but the fire within her didn't take a rest, it is working on her mind.

Humans are like this. They have this ball of fire inside them when they want things desperately or when they are so ambitious about achieving their goals.
She doesn't know what is planned for her life, but she is ready to fight for her dreams. Maybe her path could be thorny, she needs to be ready for it.
Let's read further to see what God has planned for her life.

6

The day is finally here. Lumra was waiting for this for a long. She is sitting there, scared and nervous. She frequently pats her face with a handkerchief to clean the sweat off. Zillions of thoughts are crossing her mind and suddenly she hears her name being called out. She is so anxious that she even thought of backing off but, she knows that she can't do it now.

She gets up from her seat and slowly walks onto the stage, stands in front of the microphone, clears her throat, she greets everyone.

"Hello! Good afternoon to one and all present here. My name is Lumra…..(Breathe in breathe out. You can do it, Lumra. Allah please be with me)
I am going to present my paper on…..on…(cool breeze caresses her face and gently touches her hair. She feels this is the moment she was waiting for. Please dear fear, can you wait outside for a minute, I will come for you later).

And then she talks about her topic and presents it pretty well.

Everyone applauded.

She accomplished what she wanted. Her presentation was appreciated by the mentors. She answered every question smartly.

She goes home and tells her mother how happy she is. She narrates to them lively all that happened on that particular day. They are happy for their daughter, but something was poking into her mind, that is, what happened to the proposal? She can't ask directly to her mother about this. She doesn't want to spoil her mood. So, she tries to concentrate on her studies. What is going to happen in her life she doesn't have any clue.

Wait for the progression, Lumra has yet to face many challenges and you, readers are yet to read a few more chapters.

7

In the last few weeks, owing to the conference, the classes were not taken properly. So, now all the teachers came to class to finish their portion. Lumra is tired of listening to all seminars in class and so as usual, she started dreaming about her future in her dream.

"Thank you for inviting me," Lumra says to the interviewer.

"No, it is our pleasure that you are here." The interviewer shakes hands with her and continues, "Tell me, Miss. Lumra, who inspired you? How did you achieve all these things?" The interviewer asks her.

"Selvi ma'am, my teacher in my UG programme inspired me and motivated me. My friends Grace and Shafiya are my supporting pillars. I am known for exaggerating stupid imaginations, but they bear all those stuff and supported me."

Suddenly, Shafiya shakes her and brings her back from her dream. Sr. Jasmine is standing there. Sr. Jasmine is the senior staff of the English department. Even though she does not handle class for them, they admire her a lot. Lumra is afraid of her out of respect. Sr. Jasmine is an elderly person, but she has the most vibrant personality, even if she has loads of work, she always wears a smile on her face.

"Good Morning, Sister", the whole class wished her coherently.

"Good Morning, sit down girls. I have an announcement for you all. We are invited to a conference in Chennai and I planned to take some of the UG students. I want Lumra and Grace from your class to present a paper in Chennai, I have selected a few girls from other sections too. Next week we are going to Chennai, if other girls want to join, let me know. PG girls are accompanying us and both of you prepare for your presentation. (pointingto Lumra and Grace)." After telling this Sr. Jasmine goes out. The class started their routine. Lumra is spellbound like a still night. She is astonished by what took place in front of her.

"Lumra I am happy for you", Shafiya hugs her and pokes her continuously, "Lumra…..Lumra… (Lumra sits still in her place without any movement).

"Shafiya, just tell me is that real? I feel it is surreal." Lumra asks Shafiya in an astonished tone.

"Yes, it is true Lumra. You are going to Chennai to present your paper." Shafiya says in an excited tone.

"Yes, it is true. IT IS TRUE SHAFIYA. I am really happy. Sr. Jasmine herself came and called me. I am happy but…but what if my mother doesn't allow me to go to Chennai? She never allows me to go anywhere."

Lumra is now afraid of what will happen when she discloses this to her mother.

She is always under the wings of her parents and they too never allowed her to come out from that safehold. Lumra's parents think the world outside is not safe for her, they think the society is all rotten where bringing up a girl child is a risky task, and in that they don't want to add up more risks. They think alike, one can't change society, so better keep their daughter safe, because they have a right on their daughter, not on the people of this world.

This is the mindset of every Indian family. They do the mistake of not changing their outlook because they are scared. Their prime concern is to protect their family even when the protection shield comes with its terms and conditions.

"Will you come with us?" Asks Lumra.

"They will surely allow you. Don't worry. I don't think I can come with you, because my dad is not well. I have to take care of him. But I am happy for you. I am sure that you're gonna rock." Shafiya assures her.

"Insha Allah. Take care of yourself and your father."

***

"I don't think he will be suitable for her. She is too young for him and I am not interested in this." Zainab replies on the phone.

"Yes. Tell them that we are not interested in this. Ok, thank you." Zainab turns off her mobile.

"What do you think, did I make the correct decision?" Zainab asks for assurance from her husband.

"I believe you more than myself because from their young age you only took care of them mostly and I know you don't make any decision without thinking."

Manzoor and Zainab believe in each other and that is one of the pillars on which their marriage stands successful till now.

(Lumra comes back home)

"Mom I am selected to present my papers in Chennai," Lumra tells her mother in an enthusiastic tone while her face and body language depicts how frightened she is.

"Who are all coming with you?"

"Sr. Jasmine selected some of the girls, mom."

"Even Grace is coming with me."

"For how many days?"

"It is two days program, ma."

"Hmm… Two days."Zainab thinks deeply.

"Yes, ma, I will go on Friday morning and I'll be here on Saturday night."

Allah Please make her say 'yes', Lumra prayed to the almighty.*Oh, dear heart please beat slowly, I can hear you now. I know we both are anxious, but calm down.*

After thinking for five minutes, Zainab replies, "Ok, you can go. How much does it cost?"

"Are you serious? You permitted me. Amma, I love you so much." Lumra gives a peck on her mother's cheek.

"Sr. told us to bring money for travel allowance and accommodation. She told us to bring 1500 rupees, ma."

"I will give you money. Chennai is a big city, everyone will roam here and there so, don't look at the sky and walk. Always be with your group and be careful. Ok?"

As You Wish, Mother

"Yes, ma, I'll be careful."

Lumra is very happy and she couldn't believe what just happened. Lately, Lumra's life has taken a turn. So many events are happening in her life all of a sudden. Sometimes, she pinches herself to check whether it is real or if is she dreaming.

She was never allowed to go outside alone, and for the first time in her life she is going somewhere without her parents. Even though she is excited she is not sure how will she manage without her parents. But she wants to face the world alone. So, she prepared her mind to face everything on her own and now she is going to go to Chennai. She picks up her phone and calls Grace.

"Hi, Grace! You know what! My mom allowed me to come with you guys."

"Really? Are you sure she said yes?" Grace confirms for she knows how Lumra's parents don't allow her to go to any place all alone.

"Yes. I can't believe it."

"Then we will talk to sister tomorrow, ok?"

"Ok, sure. Did your parents allow you?"

"Yes."

"Wow, that's awesome. I am excited about our journey."

"Yes, we are going to present our paper in Chennai. Oh! That's insane. I can't believe this."

"Ok, Good night. See you tomorrow."

She is confused with this series of events taking place in her life. One day it is pathetic and depressing and another day it is filled with abundant happiness. She couldn't control the unconditional joy. With this excitement, she goes to her room and writes to her friend Pinky, and sleeps cozily. She is excited about the following day unaware of what tomorrow holds in store for her.

8

"Where are they?" Manzoor asks Lumra at the railway station.

"Dad, there they are." Lumra points to a group who are gathered towards one side of the railway station. She came to this railway station many times but this time it is quite different because all this time she had traveled with her family. For the first time in her life, she is going to travel without them. This thought gave birth to both happiness and fear in her mind; she is thrilled. She never felt like this in her life.

Lumra was immersed in her thoughts.

Hey, you railway station, I know you held my feet many times but today you feel it differently because I am alone today, I am going to travel with you, without my parents. Are you excited? If no, doesn't matter to me, I am excited. I am excited as a young bird who is learning to fly, I am excited as a young infant who first sees this world. I am excited as...

"COME FAST." Her father's yelling brings her back from the labyrinth of her thoughts.

"Yes, Dad!" She walks behind him and she sees her friends standing in front of the ticket booking center.

"Lumra! Go fast to get your ticket from that counter", says one of her classmates.

In her life she has never stood in a queue for a ticket, her father only gets tickets for them and it is quite uneasy for her. But this time, even Manzoor lets her buy the ticket.

"Always be with your group and your teacher. Be careful. All the best." Manzoor pats her back and leaves for his work.

Tears starts rolling down her eyes as Manzoor left the station.She closes her eyes for a moment, consoles herself, and walks towards the queue.

She saw a girl in the queue and stands behind her, she

identified that girl, she is from the same college but a different section.

"Hi, I am Vinaya. You too are from our college, right?" She extends her hand to Lumra.

"Yes. My name is…."

"Lumra, I know!"

"How do you know?" Lumra asks surprisingly.

"Well…You are quite famous. I saw your presentation at the conference and that was nice. Since then, you are the talk of the department.

"Thank you!" Lumra blushed a little and to avoid the awkward silence she asked her fellow mate, "You too presented your paper, right?"

"Yes, I did. But, yours was superb."

"Thank you."

"Can I get a ticket for the three of us? And by the way, she is Yamini, my friend." She introduces the girl who stands beside her.

"Hi, Yamini (she extends her hand to Yamini), thank you but my friend Grace still didn't arrive. Can we wait for her?"

Here she comes, Grace runs towards Lumra.

"Hi! Lumra sorry…(exhales) a littlebit…(exhales) late." She breathes heavily.

"Calm down. Here, have some water." Lumra gives her the bottle and continues, "This is Vinaya and this is Yamini. They are from our college and are accompanying us."

"Hi Girls. I am Grace. Nice to meet you! Did you all get tickets?" Grace asks them hurriedly.

"No, we were waiting for you." Says Lumra.

Yamini gets the tickets for everyone. Sr. Jasmine calls everyone to gather so that they can head toward the platform together.

"The train will arrive here in half an hour. So, all of you wait here", says Sr. Jasmine.

"You did your presentation perfectly, then why were you frightened in the beginning? We both prayed for you (Yamini points out to Vinaya) but after that. OH MY... unbelievable, you nailed it!!!"

"Thank you. I was afraid because it was my first-ever presentation. Even Grace was not with me at that time to motivate me, but that was a great experience, I can't forget that day."

All the students were talking to one another while they were waiting for their train to arrive.

"Hey look, the train is almost here", one of her classmates points to the train which was quite at a distance.

As the train reached the station, the girls started to jump in excitement. On the other hand, Sr. Jasmine checked whether everyone is present or not.

OK, tell me says Vinaya. *Their conversation continues once again and there is no end to it. It goes on but it ends abruptly when they reach Chennai.*

This is the first time Lumra is visiting Chennai. She sees this big city with lots of people busy traveling. She is amused by how early morning, people are running here and there when she saw a group of people running behind the bus to board it. She feels how can they all live here. She was never exposed to this environment before. Even though in Vellore she saw many people travel climbing on the footboard, this was quite different. Sr. Jasmine rechecked whether everyone was present there. A sister comes and she leads them to a yellow van, they get into the van.

"Hello friends, my name is Sr. Danielle. I welcome you all to Chennai. I'll try to make this travel a memorable one for all of you, enjoy your journey."
They reached a building that is a school and Sr. Danielle leads them. They go to a basement of an auditorium, which is a massive hall.

"Girls, be ready. We are going to the conference at 10'o clock," and she leaves them.

These entire things were new to Lumra but she starts to enjoy them. She loves the place. She takes a bath and wears a pink salwar, white leggings, and a white shawl. All of them gather in front of the school and climb into the van. When they reach the spot all are astonished by the huge buildings. It was an old building but it has an elegant look. They enter the building which had huge banners hanging all around it, and sculptures of famous personalities. The ceiling was breathtaking. Lumra was in awe.

Sr. Jasmine asks for the route to the conference hall four students from there lead them. They enter the hall and reach the place on time and register themselves. The first day was ordinary and they talk about many theories and some of the officials from other countries present their papers. Lumra enjoyed that day a lot.

They went in search of a restaurant to have lunch in but couldn't find any nearby the building. So they, walk for around a kilometer or two and find one.
Suddenly Vinaya realized that Sr. Danielle who accompanied them is not with them. Vinaya called her and she replied that she is stuck somewhere. Everyone is tired so Vinaya stands alone not knowing what to do.

"Hi Vinaya, what happened? Why didn't you come to eat?"

"Lumra, Sr. Dannielle is stuck on the other side and she wants someone to direct her to this place."

"Can I accompany you?"

"If you are ok then I am happy about it."

And both of them move ahead.

"Sir, where is the Sangam textile?" Vinaya asked a stranger.

"Go straight at the end of the road you will find it."

"Is it too far, sir?

"No, it's not long you can reach that place in five minutes."

"Thank you, sir."

"Oh my, is this that five minutes, we are walking for at least half an hour."

"Yes, Lumra. I am thirsty now. I think we will become old in five minutes. Shall we confirm once again where is the correct location? What do you think?"

"Me too. Wait we will ask someone."

Lumra goes to a shop which was on her left-hand side.

As You Wish, Mother

She asks the shopkeeper about the distance from the given location.

"What did he say?"

"What do you think?"

"Same five minutes. Ughhh," and they laughed together.

After walking for five minutes, they finally reached their destination. They hugged each other in joy.

"Sr. Dannielle, we reached the place. Where are you?"

"I can see you. Wait I am coming." Sr. Dannielle takes a breath. "Girls, can we go now? Is it a walkable distance or should we take an auto?"

"It's hardly five minutes." Lumra and Vinaya say together and starts laughing.

"Better to take an auto."

They attend the afternoon session. Their first day went well. They returned to their place, and while their travel they bought food for dinner. The route is quite narrow, so Sr. Danielle prefers the walk. They walk slowly. Lumra leads her students with Sr. Danielle. The place is quite beautiful even though it is filled with rushing bikes and cars. While reaching the convent it is nearly 9'O clock at night, everyone is tired but that didn't make them weak. All of them refreshed themselves and eat together, they dance and sing and watch films at night.

This is one of the finest days Lumra ever has.

The next day they all wake up early, and they feel very weight-hearted because this is the last day of their trip. Even though they stayed only one night in that place, it makes them feel at home, they take pictures of that place for their memory and bid farewell to that place very sadly. When they come out of the school, students were having their morning prayer. Lumra recollects all her childhood memories, in her school days she never spoke in front of her class, and she never pulled herself forward but now, she is in Chennai to present her paper. She feels proud of herself. She never imagined such drastic changes to be happening in her life. She feels like how a butterfly works hard to come out from a caterpillar for the first time after a long struggle, likewise, she can now spread her wings, even if it is not big but efforts matter.

The second day or the last day of their conference started. Today, Lumra is going to present her paper. Like in her college, it is also a success, she takes all of her points and landed them very smoothly then she answered all questions very elegantly. This time she didn't feel low, she knows she can do it, she pulls herself forward and believed in herself, delivered her presentation well.

In the afternoon session, they invited one of the popular authors named Rekha, Lumra doesn't know about her visit when she knows it, and she is very happy about it. Because she listened to almost all of her interviews and she loves her writing too.

"Hello students, I am addressing you first because you are the future and here I am honored to invite the future of our world." The author gives her motivational speech with utmost grace and confidence which makes the audience astonished.

After her speech, one of the listeners asks, "From where do you get inspiration to write?"

"My life is my story I don't want any muse to amuse me to write a novel or short story. I meet many people in my daily life who carry some stories, I take all of their stories and combine them with mine, then I deliver them with some interesting ideas. That's it. There is no need for one to experience adventurous things to write a novel. All of your life contains a story if you brush it with some fictional imagination and present it to the world. They all love it. All you need is passion and patience to write it and bring it to print media."

As soon as the question session with the author gets over, Lumra's friends run behind the author to get her autograph.

Lumra stands still in that place, she is affected by her speech, she recalls her speech again and again in her mind because whatever she writes, be it poetry or short story, it has a trace of her personal experience. She writes all that to erase the unwanted memories and sometimes to store all that makes her happy. She never thought that could be also considered work.

Someone's touch on her shoulder interrupts her thoughts, She turns around only to get surprised.

The hand on her shoulder belongs to none other than the author herself.

"I like your presentation, it was very lively." Lumra has butterflies in her stomach but she controlled her emotions and says,
"Thank you, ma'am, it means a lot to me."

"I like the way you presented it. It was not common, it has some personal touch that connects everyone."

"Thank you." She struggles a little and asks her, "Can I ask you something?"

"Yes. What do you want to ask?" She asks Lumra calmly.

"You said that all our life contains a story that should be told, but how my story will connect to others? All that I feel or experience may not be understood by people the way I understood or the way it affects me. Then how it could connect with others?

"Yes, your life is different from others, you may think that your life is boring but believe me, through your words you can give strength to someone who is in need, at that very particular moment. Your story need not be adventurous but your story should have the connectivity which brings your reader to your position. You are bringing some element to your story that makes the story more beautiful. Don't think that your story will not connect with people. Be true to your emotions, and tell what you want to express. If you are true to yourself your story will speak many things. You never knew what changes you can bring into people's life. I hope you got your answer."

"Yes. Thank you, ma'am."

"And I believe you can become a good writer. Are you interested in writing?"

"Yes, I am interested in writing, but not sure whether I can be a good writer."

"Yes, definitely you can. All the best." The author takes a leave from there.

Lumra is standing there and all she could think is about the advice she just now got from her favorite author.

"Hello! Everyone is gone, why are you standing here?" She shrugged because of the sudden voice then she realized that she is standing alone in that conference hall. "Answer me," asks Yamini another time.

"Nothing, I just spoke with the chief guest."

"What? Did you just speak to her?"

"Yes, I did." And with all the joy in her heart, she tells Yamini about her and the chief guest's conversation. It was late, so they both run to join their group.

✸✸✸

They are now on the outer side of the college, expecting the van as they have to leave. Sr. Jasmine will meet them at the railway station, she couldn't accompany them because of some other meeting in Chennai. Sr. Danielle is with them.

"Girls, you are in Chennai and how could you miss Marina Beach? So we are now heading towards Marina beach and then we will go to the railway station. OK?"

"Yes." They all answered.

All of them go to the beach and start to play in the wide ocean. Lumra now sees all things differently. This wide ocean paves a way for Lumra to play without any limitations, for the first time in her life she breathes the free air. She feels free, she feels like no one can stop her, for the first time she feels that she is living in this world, for the first time she wants to shout *"Dear world, I am alive, can you feel me?"*

She never feels this kind of happiness in her life. She just wants to fly now, she wants to tell everyone that she is one among them. She expressed all her emotions with the ocean, even the ocean plays with her. They both join together and play a lot. She feels like an infant for the first time who sees the world. Every journey has an end, and so does this.

In Vellore, her family and her life waiting for her. In Chennai she has abundant memories that make her strong, this experience proved to her that she is also capable of something and she too can achieve something in her life. With all these memories she starts her travel to Vellore, where many twists and turns are waiting for her.

"Hello, tell me?"

"Oh! Yes. What is he doing?"

"When are they planning to come? Because my daughter is not here, she went to Chennai she will come tomorrow so tell them to come, the day after tomorrow."

"We will make sure what should be done on our side, Yes, I will tell him."

Zainab turns towards Manzoor and tells him, "Azeema told me that she knows her neighbor who wants to see our daughter. That guy is working in some company it seems and she told that he is a good fellow. So, I told her to bring their family the day after tomorrow."

"Ok, just get their address if we are interested we will check about their family background."

"Ok, I will ask her all about it and I think that it's better we don't tell Lumra about this. Better she goes to college as usual and we will disclose this after she comes home. What do you say?"

"Even I think it is better."

I think this is life. There Lumra just found what she needs to do in her future, but here Zainab got one proposal for her daughter's fairytale future. That's why I don't like the irony of life which always gives happiness with the pain. Let's see what happens.

9

"I think this is one of the most memorable travels I ever have. What do you think, Grace?"

"Yes, the same. I saw a new version of you in Chennai and I am really happy about it. You know, in Chennai, you were open and adventurous. There I saw the thirst you have for life and how you're longing to live happily and freely."

"Yes, Grace, even I am thinking the same. I scrutinize myself in Chennai. I never knew that I am capable of this much. Now I know that I can speak fluently, I know that I can present papers well, and I get to know many things about myself in Chennai. I will never forget all those experiences."

All the parents were coming to pick up their daughters.

"There is my dad." Lumra enthusiastically shows her father to her friends and goes near him. Lumra bid farewell to her friends and went with her father. Lumra reaches home. She is desperate to talk to her parents. She couldn't hold her tongue for a moment. Because she has so many things to tell about the journey which made her strong. The journey mirrors who she is, the journey that gives her the confidence to face the world. Both Zainab and Manzoor lend their ears to Lumra to finish her story. Then she starts to narrate this to her brother and she goes to sleep; she is also very excited about her class tomorrow. Without knowing what they have planned for her tomorrow.

"Congrats! Lumra."

"What for, Shafiya?"

"Grace told me that you were rocking in Chennai. I missed you all and I missed your presentation too."

"Even I missed you Shafiya and thank you for your compliments."

"Tell me about your experience. I want to hear it from you."

"I am ready to tell you, but if you feel bored or if your ears start to bleed then I am not responsible. Is that ok with you?"

"Yes. I am ok with it." (They both laugh)

And Lumra starts to narrate everything that happened in Chennai. Shafiya gets to know how much she enjoyed her trip by the spark in her eyes and her exciting tone.

Everyone who enters the classroom congratulates Lumra and Grace for their presentation. Lumra felt happy about all of this. During break time, everyone was talking to each other. She saw Grace and Shafiya talking about something very serious and she ventures into her world; she recalled the speech of that author and their conversation. All those moments were magical and that made her happy.

She feels that she should stand on her own before getting married, she doesn't want to be ordinary. She wants to become a writer because she knows that she is only good at writing, then she wants to make her parents proud. She wants to make her parents popular and she wants to give all the happiness to them through her victory.

As You Wish, Mother

"Mom, I am here."

"Lumra, wash your hair and wear the dress I kept on the table."

Lumra gets what is happening, but she can't digest the thing that her mother allowed a man who is much older than her. She obeys her mother and goes to take a bath. Her heart sinks and is ready to break into numerous pieces but she kept silent. What can she do? When were women allowed to say "NO" in this world? Lumra is no exception.

When are they coming? Yes, she is getting ready. dear, did you buy some sweets?

Lumra hears the faded voices of her mother. She doesn't want to cry, because she knows that her mother doesn't like this. She prays to Allah to give strength to her.
"Allah, I cannot hold this. Why….Why this happens to me all the time? Can't I taste happiness in my life? Is it a sin to be happy? What sin did I commit to sufferlike this? I know many people want to get married in the

world but I am not one of them, you know that, then why? Just now I got some idea to flourish in my life and here? You are showing me the way and at the same time giving me the obstacle...I can't bear this. Please help me."

Tears roll down her face, her eyes are swollen even though she is underwater, her lips are dry. She could feel the pain in her heart and it throbs.

"Lumra, are you ready?" She gains consciousness and replies to her mother, (washes her face, cleared her throat) "Yes, Amma."

Her aunt comes to her home and puts makeup on her face. She looks like an angel but the irony here is this angel's heart had already been dead. This is just a corpse. Yes, Lumra didn't show any feelings on her face, because she is very conscious of controlling her tears which are ready to come out at any time.

"Get inside... Get inside they are coming. Her mother tells her aunt and they send Lumra to one room. She is sitting there alone. Lumra tries her best to control her tears. She hears many noises, but she is not interested in their talk.

Oh, he just now finished his degree, I mean two years back, and by Allah's Grace, he got a job in Chennai.

Now she gets to know that he is not that person her mother talked about. Even though he is young, she doesn't feel anything towards that unknown fellow. No one ever attracted her the way books do.

He is head of the company, a very hard-working fellow, even he is not ready for marriage we only pushed him and got his permission.

She just feels weak. She hears moving chair sounds, by this time she knew that they are coming for her because this is not the first time people visiting her to make her their bride. She wipes her eyes and sits still in her place. A group of people enters her room. She sees an elderly woman who has nearly crossed fifty, two middle-aged women and their children (she guessed). One of the middle-aged women volunteers her talk, "I am the groom's sister, she is his sister-in-law and they are our children, she introduces everyone.She is the groom's mother," and she directs towards the elderly woman who is sitting in front of her. They start to analyzeLumra, they tell her to stand and the groom's sister calculates her height. They ask Lumra some questions and she answers all of them politely and then she becomes quiet. They laughed at themselves with their lame jokes.

"Is she always quiet?"

"No not like that, you all are new to her that's why or else she would have talked a lot." Zainab defends her daughter.

"What are you studying?" An elderly woman asks Lumra. When the topic changes to education, her voice breaks without her control but she tried to control that and replies, "**B.A. English**."

Then they go outside and her mother asks many things about their family, especially about the groom. Manzoor too asks some questions to one man that should be the groom's father. After all these conversations they left the house.

This was the first time Lumra first time feels betrayed. She never thought that her mother could do something like this. She entered home thinking that she could share all incidents that happen today but all her expectations were drowned when she enters the home.

She felt like everything was going to change, but she didn't expect much change. Her mother called her to have dinner. She thought of sharing all her joy at dinner time but now she shared her silence. Her brother without considering anything munches his food and eats normally. Her parents also eat without speaking.
After everyone finished their dinner she cleanses the table and washes dishes, her mother goes to sleep.
Lumra sobs while washing dishes. Her cheeks and nose become red. And her eyes, looks as if they are bleeding.

She goes to her room, picks up her diary and pen, and starts writing. While writing her tears gushes out from her eyes, and all the tears she controlled the whole evening rolled over from her eyes. She asks herself why all these happenings happen in her life.

Dear Pinky,

I don't know who is wrong. Is that me or my mom? She can't be wrong because she never thinks of anything that could hurt me. But why couldn't I accept this thing, even though I know she is always right. Is anything wrong with me? Allah, please help me, I don't know what to do. But I am sure I don't want to marry now I have many things to do if you think I should marry now, I better die. I can't leave my dream and live alone. If this is my fate, then I guess, it is better for me to sleep, forever. I don't want this life, please take it away from me. Allah. I don't think I will accept that life, for now, it's hurting, it's painful. Show me some way so that I can escape. If this going to happen then please let me close my eyes and not open them at all. Let me open my eyes in the morning only if it is not going to happen. You know what I mean... this... this marriage thing is not on my list, at least not for now.

She finishes writing and tries to sleep. She knows that this night is going to be hard but she never thought that it could be this hard.

✳✳✳

Meanwhile, Zainab is crying while sleeping. Manzoor hears her weeping so he turns toward her and asks her, "What happened? Why are you crying it happens most of the time, you know that, right?" Zainab wipes off her tears.

"I know, she does this every time. But she was younger

then, now she is not the same. She should change and she can't be like this always."

"The mistake is with us, we never teach her anything, anything about the world, she only knows about her studies. Rather than studies, we should have taught her how to live in this cruel world."

"Yes, that is correct. Butwhy is she like this, she is very sensitive towards everything that is not at all good for her. There are many people outside to put her down, she can't hold the betrayal of someone. I don't want her to be anxious, that's why I didn't tell her about this proposal. Now she will think that I am hiding everything from her."

"No, she will not think like that, she knows about her mother and our daughter is a good one. She is precious. You know that. Allah will take care of her."

"When she is going to realize that we are not going to leave her alone. We won't choose someone who is not at all good to her. We care about her future a lot more than her. When is she going to understand that?"

"She knew everything, don't worry about her. She

believes you a lot and she knows whatever you do is for her good. Don't disturb yourself thinking about all this, sleep now."

Though Zainab closes her eyes; she doesn't feel sleepy, she thinks about Lumra.

I think this is the war between both mother and daughter, where they care for one another but fails to understand their dreams. Here no one is wrong and that is the pathetic situation. If someone is wrong it is easy to point them out, but here who is wrong? The daughter who just wants to accomplish her dream or the mother who is seeking the best future for her daughter? Think about it. Now, what will happen in their life?
It is a mystery that needed to be unveiled still.

10

After that day, Lumra became very quiet, she does not talk athome. She has now become reserved and silent. Even if everyone is talking to her at home, she does not respond. She feels, if she behaves like this they may try to break this proposal, but they will not. She tries to find various reasons to stay away from the house.

Mom, I have a special class. So, I'll come late,
Mom, ma'am gave me some work. So, I'll stay at college. Mom, I am going to stay at college to study.

She gives all the possible lame excuses to stay away from home. Because she feels like she is surrounded by melancholy when she is at home. She wants to cry and on the other hand, she doesn't want to hurt her mother.

Nowadays, Zainab has stopped talking to her. Even if Lumra initiated the conversation, Zainab just cuts it off with small phrases. She can bear the scolding of her mother, not her silence, her heart begs for her mother's love. She missed her mother so much. When she realizes that she will not talk to her, she just wants to stay away from her because she thought she is the reason for her mother's miserable state. She separated herself from her mother. Both Zainab and Lumra's relationship is sinking, but both are striving hard to stabilize their relationship. To stabilize a relationship someone should sacrifice their dreams, but both are rigid in their own decision.

It has been a week since she spoke properly in college. Lumra loses herself in her own thoughts while everyone is going for a break. Everyone asks her what has happened to her, and she just replies to them that she is not well and continues her work. Even some of the professors enquire about her but she just gives them some lame excuses and runs away. Shafiya notices her behavior, but she is waiting for one perfect moment to ask her when she sees that Lumra is alone in the classroom and this is the moment she was waiting for.

"What happened to you? After coming from Chennai

you are not fine? You are behaving very strangely. Did something happen in Chennai?"

"Nothing, Shafiya! I am ok. Just not feeling well that's it."

"Do you think I don't know you? I know how you react when you are sick physically. It's not a physical sickness, it is a emotional sickness. Tell me what happened. If you will talk, only then I can give some solution. Even if I can't give a solution, you may feel better after you disclose it. I am not pushing you to tell, if you are not willing to, it is ok. Just believe I am here for you all the time."

Lumra broke her silence, tears rushing down from her eyes, she wipes out her tears and starts to narrate the event that happened a week before and how there is a split between her mother. She pours out everything which she is holding for a week.

"Lumra I know you are hurt, but you should think about your parents too. Look, they are aged and they are afraid of what will happen to you after them." Shafiya tries to explain to her.

"Do you think I don't know about that? I know how they spent their life on me and Suhail. Do you know what is my dream? I want to make them happy. I want to give them all the happiness, the way they have showered all happiness in my life. I don't believe in this patriarchal rule where they say boys should take care of their parents. I am the elder one in the family so I am the one who is responsible for them. That's why I don't want to get married now. I need to accomplish many things in life."

"I can understand your feelings, but crying in front of others may create embarrassment to your parents, why are you crying? Do you think your parents will choose someone who is not suitable for you? They will find a suitable person for you. It's not that they find someone good and they will get you married the next day, it's a long process."

"I know about that, but I hate these customs. Sometimes it sucks, I am afraid, I don't know why? I feel alone and helpless when people come. I don't know how to express it. This time I tried my best. I controlled my emotions. But, my mother failed to recognize it. These days I feel irritated when someone talks about marriage and I prayed to Allah that this proposal should break, if not I don't know what will happen." She sobs.

"Are you mad? One shouldn't pray for such things. It is God who decides our fate. What if he wants you to get married? Will you go against God's will? Or do you plan to live alone without getting married? Do you think your parents will leave you alone?" Shafiya yelled at her.

"Even I don't want to pray like this, but I am afraid, what to do? what will happen after marriage? From the moment I was born to this moment I depend on my parents, I do whatever they order me to do.Do you think I don't have anything on my own? I want to live my life. I don't want to lose it. I don't want to depend on someone after marriage too. I want my own space to live, I want to smile the way I want, I want to jump the way I want, I want to do things the way I want. I feel caged. It is always painful." Lumra's voice breaks. She is hurt. She wipes off her tears with her dupatta and says, "You know, I love my mom abundantly, my mom suffered a lot and she faced many criticisms from the family yet she gives us the best in everything. I want to do something for her. I want to give her all the love. But I feel like she hates me now, she doesn't talk

As You Wish, Mother

to me nowadays. I don't want this separation between us. I am afraid that I will lose her and this feeling gives me more pain. I can't bear this Shafiya." Lumra couldn't control her emotions anymore. She puts her head on Shafiya's shoulder and weeps.

The bell rings for their next class.

"Oh dear, don't cry. Allah is watching you. He will take care of you. Shed no more tears now. Be attentive in class."

Lumra nods and goes to her class along with her friend.

Lumra loves to study. If there were no lecture, she would have been weeping till now. The fictional worlds written by the authors distracted her for an entire hour. She is not crying anymore.

"Hey, Shafiya. What if I call them and tell them that I am not interested? And tell them to tell my mother that they are not interested in this proposal."

"Do you think they will leave this matter just like that? They will talk to your parents and for your information, this is not a movie this is reality. One can't do like this."

"Yeah, I know, but what if some miracle happens? What if they feel I am not good-looking and they feel like… I am not suitable for them? I will be very happy, I don't feel bad if they say I am not good-looking."

"Lumra! Don't get anxious! Allah will take care of everything."

"I trust only him. I can't ask for anything but to get rid away of this proposal."

"What if it is for your good?"

"I am ready to face the consequences."

***

"What happened? Do you think they are good for Lumra?" Asks Azeema about the recent proposal which came for Lumra.

As You Wish, Mother

"I am not sure, I feel they are good, but still, it is about Lumra. So, I want to be more careful about that. I told some of my relatives to check on them."

"That is correct. But, then why do you look so sad?"

"I am thinking about Lumra. I don't know what she is thinking."

"She is still a child that is all I can tell. Don't think about her now. Everything will become normal when she gets married. We are all like that, you know how much I cried before marriage, but see, everything has changed and so will she."

"But, Lumra is not like that. She loves to study, she is really afraid of this relationship, she thinks that I don't know her. But, I know her well. She is very innocent."

"You are telling me that you know her, then why it makes you sad? She is a good girl. Don't worry she will be fine in a few days. Did she cry this time too?"

"Yes, she did cry. She didn't understand what it causes her. She feels if she cries they won't accept her. But, when she cries they think something is wrong with her

As You Wish, Mother

and after their arrival, she became very quiet at home, she even didn't talk to me properly, I feel I lost my daughter." Zainab is almost in tears.

"Don't cry, pray to Allah, he will take care of everything. Don't think about her. If you find this proposal good for her then let her get married. We should only think about their future, no one is going to care about their future except for us. She is your child you have the right to make a wise decision about her life. She doesn't know anything about life. So, she should obey your decision.
Be strong for her."

✳✳✳

"Lumra wear a proper dress!" Zainab enters the home suddenly.
Lumra feels something wrong, and suddenly, the elderly woman who came to visit her the other day enters her home.

"It's ok! Leave her. After marriage, she will be like this in our home. And she looks beautiful in any dress." Says the woman.

I am not going to get married now. Don't imagine a lot, dear elder woman. Allah, please I can't face this moment. Make her leave this place as soon as possible.

"How are you Lumra?" She asks.

"Fine." Her voice is heavy and her eyes are numb.

"I came nearby for some work, so thought of seeing our Lumra. It is like our home too, right?"

"Yes, it is." Said Zainab with a smile.

They had a long conversation. An hour later, the woman realizes that it's getting late.

"Wait some more time. Why don't you have dinner with us and then you can go."

"Not today, Zainab. Some other day for sure I will have dinner with you. If you don't mind, can I come here to visit Lumra whenever I feel like?"

"Yes, yes. You can come whenever you want. This is your home too."

The woman kisses Lumra on her forehead and bids her goodbye.

"Lumra, clean the house." Zainab orders.

Lumra is confused and in panic. "Why this woman wants to visit me whenever she wishes to?" She murmurs.

"Aunt Mehboob and Uncle Zakeer are visiting our home. They are coming to invite us to Mariyam's wedding."

Lumra knows Mariyam, she is a doctorate scholar in her thirties. While she was studying she did not think of marriage. Apart from books, there was nothing on her mind. Lumra is jealous of her sometimes, for she thinks about how her mother allowed her to achieve her dreams and here, Zainab wants her to get married as soon as possible. One will fall in love with Mariyam as soon as oneseeher. She is happy that Mariyam is now getting married but she is worried. She knows that they will talk about her marriage, and thinking about those things makes her tensed but she obeys her mother and cleans her home.

They arrived at their home and they were talking about the groom and Mehaboob goes to the kitchen where Zainab is cooking for them.

"How are you, Zainab?It's been a long time since we've met."

"Yeah. On some occasions only we get a chance to visit. In the race of earning money, there is no time to visit one another."

"That is correct. I want to ask you one thing, is there anything wrong with Lumra? Why is she quiet?"

"Nothing, a proposal came and that's why she is behaving like this."

"Lumra is very sensitive. I think."

"Yes, she is. That's why I am worried about her."

"I just want to tell you one thing. There is a proper time for everything and we should think about that, I did a mistake by listening to Mariyam and her wish, but now it's been a hard time for us to find a groom. Our daughters are still a child to us, but there is something called age, we should think about that. Just think about her future that is important to us."

***

Lumra meets Shafiya in college and tells her about the sudden visit of that woman.

"What? You were not wearing any make-up when she came. And you were in casuals." Shafiya was shocked for some reason,

"Yes."

"I can't even imagine that. Yesterday my aunt came to visit me, but I wore good clothes."

"She was there out of nowhere. And she told that she had some work nearby so she thought of visiting me. I mean, our families are not even close, she should at least have informed us."

"She must have wanted to meet her future daughter-in-law." Safiya teases her.

"Do not put that label on me, Shafiya," Lumra says strictly. She is irritated.

All of us in this world are assigned some work, we just want relief from that work, so we try to accomplish it as soon as possible. I don't say it is wrong, but that work should finish wholeheartedly, not half finish, and have happiness on one side. I don't know why I am telling this. Let's continue our story.

As You Wish, Mother

11

Zainab is very disappointed since the visit of Mehboob and Zakeer. She feels like her daughter insulted her in front of them, being very adamant in the house when the outsiders are at home.

Lumra is cleaning the table while her mother is sitting on the sofa, deeply lost in her thoughts.

"Mom, do you want something?" Lumra asks politely.

"I want to speak with you, come and sit next to me." Says Zainab.

Lumra's heart starts to beat fast. She just hates this moment. She knows what is going to happen next. She doesn't know how she is going to face her mother, she can't speak anything in front of her mother, and she knows somehow her mother will prove that she is correct whereas, her dear daughter is being stubborn for no reason. At worse, she will see her mother cry, she hates when her mother cries because of her. But, she cannot do anything now so, she goes near to her mother and sits in front of her.

"Tell me what is the problem with you? Why are you behaving so strangely these days?"

"Nothing mom, I am perfectly alright."

"Do you think I don't know anything about you? I gave birth to you and I know how you are by looking at you."

Then why don't you understand that I hate marriage and love to study?

"No ma, nothing, I am perfectly fine."

"I know you are like this because of that proposal. Do you think I will make the wrong decision for you and your life? If yes, tell me. I will never take any decision." Zainab's anger is at its peak, her cheeks flushed and her eyes shed tears full of love and care.

"Mom, I believe you a lot, you were the reason for my birth and this life. You love me more than anyone in the world, I know that and you will never take any wrong action when it comes to my life."

"Then why are you stubborn about this thing and why are you behaving strangely when someone visits our home? You know what Mehaboob asked me, she asked what happen to you. Can't you understand that you, yourself are letting people create the wrong mindset about you?

"Mom, I am what I am. I am not behaving strangely."

"You are not Lumra, my daughter Lumra is changed now. She has lost her faith in me. I believed that she understands me, but now she too fails to understand me and now I don't have anyone in the world."
Seeing her mother cry because of her is the hardest thing for Lumra.

"Mom, you are the only one I can believe in this world, you even take care of small things related to me, I know that and you are more conscious about my marriage too. But…"

"What but?" Zainab calms herself down. "Lumra, if you believe me then why can't you tell me, "I believe you and I will obey you", why can't you tell me that? Is it so hard for you?"

"Mom, it is not about trust. I just want to work and make my own identity, so that there is no need for me to depend on someone." Finally, Lumra says what she wants to tell.

"What are you talking about Lumra? Standing on your own and not depending on someone will break your relationship. When you get married you both should depend on one another.If you think like this your life will be vanquished. Do you know, apart from studies there are more things in life which are important. Can I tell you something? You know Mariyam, right? She too talked about creating an identity and stuff like that, but what happened to her, she is going to get married and live with her husband. That is life! In her search for an identity, she lost her age, and her parents have money, so there is no problem for her. Here, the situation is different. We are struggling here for our daily allowance. You can acquire knowledge even after you become old, but marriage, it is something that should be done at the right time. And that right time for you is NOW." Zainab stretched on 'NOW'. "As you will age, it will become hard for us to find a groom, in this age only they will search for a bride, after some years we need to search. It is not that I feel you are a burden. I can very well leave you just like that but life is complex, it is hard to survive in this world. This is the right age, so when you get married, the suffering you will undergo will dissolve at your young age and you will get mature by the time. Even if you think that I am troubling you, I am going to do what is good for you. That's it." Without waiting for Lumra's response, Zainab leaves the room.

Lumra feels guilty for her doings, but she believes her decision is correct. She cannot stand the fact that why her mother fails to see her vision. And she asks herself, why she couldn't say, "AS YOU WISH, MOTHER". This night is a hard one for both mother and daughter.

Why this marriage becomes a barrier to every woman, it creates a hole between my mother and me. I love my mother. I want to be a reason for her happiness, not her sadness, why can't a girl child fulfill the dream of her parents? Does this world still think that the girl child is an extra load; a burden? Allah, please help me. I don't know what to do.

As You Wish, Mother

✳✳✳

Lumra is quiet in the class as always, Shafiya sits next to her and asks her if she's fine or not.

"Yesterday, my mom spoke with me about marriage."

"What did she say?"

Lumra tells her everything without a pause.

"Lumra you should think on behalf of your mother too, she too has some work, in that sense, you should be her caretaker, not her pain giver. I am sorry for this, but if you need to study; Allah is there, he will take care of that don't worry."

"My mom gave me a letter today morning."

"What is that letter about?" Shafiya asks in concern.

"She said in the letter that she is going to that groom's home today and some of our relatives will also accompany her."

"Lumra just believe in Allah, he is there, and he will take care of everything."

As You Wish, Mother

Lumra,

This is your mom. I never thought that your marriage will give me a hard time and I never thought I will go against you. I thought that my daughter will believe me and accept whatever I choose for her. In my life, I faced many challenges, but this is quite hard for me. For me, you and Suhail are my world. For you alone, I am living. I don't know whether you were aware that your father is not interested in your higher studies, I am the one who convinced him, but today, you have disappointed me. I never expected this from you. After my marriage, I faced many troubles and got insulted many times in front of our relatives, I worked so hard to prove them wrong and I create a higher standard in front of them, that is all for you and your brother. When you are not aware of it, it gives me pain. Even though my journey is very tough and tiring, I did that for your happiness. You are my happiness. I just want to see you both leading a beautiful life, is that wrong? Even if that is wrong I don't care. I know one day you will realize your mother is correct.

You are now living in the cinematic world and you are influenced by movies and novels, I knew that by our yesterday's conversation. Whatever you see in the movie and read in books is not reality Lumra, just be practical.

Even though you are not interested I am going to that groom's place to visit them. Let's see what Allah's plan is.

With love,
Your Mother.

After reading the letter, she couldn't stay in her classroom, she just wants to burst out, she wants to cry her heart out, and she waits until the class ends. As soon as the bell rings, she takes away all her belongings and goes to her home. On her way she just has numerous unanswered questions.

How can she say that what I feel and say is fictional and cinematic? Can't a real person have those feelings? Can only a married woman live a happy life? Am I incapable of understanding my mother? Is there any unwritten law that says that a girl child should only think about growing a family and not guard her parents and follow her passion?

She has still more questions, but she couldn't think about that now. Because now she just wants to cry, she doesn't have anyone to talk with. When she reaches her home she directly goes to her bathroom. She realizes that she is alone in her home. She doesn't care about this now, she opens the tap and splashes the fresh running water on her face, the coolness of the water this time losing its power to cool her mind, with her fiery tears even the cold water starts to spread heat. For the first time in three years she has cried loudly, she never cries like this. But, now she should pour her heart out. She never tries to control her tears, it starts to fall without any barrier, her heart sinks into pieces, and she remembers all the words written by her mother, her mother told her to tear the paper, and she tears the paper, but now all those words were written in her heart, which cannot be erased. She is crying and crying.

What happened there? Is this an end to her studies? What will happen in her future? Is there anything called the future? Why can she not accept the fact that there are some people out there, were successful in their life after marriage? Is she right or wrong? Will her mother love her the way she always did? How can she survive if her mother hates her? Thinking all about this she cries more. She slowly goes near her table and

As You Wish, Mother

starts writing to Pinky. Once she is done writing, she places Pinky in her bedside drawer.
She buried her face in her pillow and starts to cry, her pillow is now filled with her tears and gradually she goes to sleep.

I just don't want to wake up if I am going to get married and take my life from this body so that everyone will be happy, I know my mother will cry, but it is ok to cry some days than cry eternally because of me. I am sure if I get married I will not lead a happy life, I will die in thin. Allah, please help me I am not able to carry this pain. It is aching to the core.

Zainab comes home, she finds Lumra sleeping in her room, and she gently touches her hair and finds her pillow soaked in tears.
Lumra feels someone touching and she finds that it is none other than her mother. She doesn't want to open her eyes because she has already lost all her strength. She doesn't have any more strength to face her mother another time.

A mother-and-daughter relationship has been successfully ruined.

I couldn't find any mistake in both of them, why this destiny works like this I don't have any idea. Some people want to marry and lead a beautiful life they don't have that option and here's the opposite.

12

"How can they talk about our daughter like that? What did they know about her? This is our mistake, without knowing about them we went to their house." Zainab says to Manzoor in a high-pitched voice.

The parents are worried. They can't believe that they were such people. They are still talking about the incident which happened at the guy's house.

"It is not our mistake. Thank Allah that he showed their real colors to us before anything could happen with our daughter."

"That is correct. But from now on we should check thoroughly on the family before deciding anything and we should tell them to continue our daughter's studies because she loves to study. I can't see my daughter crying all the time." This time Zainab is serious.

"We will do that and you don't need to worry about our daughter. Allah will take care of her. We know about our daughter there is no need for others to give credit for our daughter's behavior."

Zainab reminds herself of how tragic her daughter looked yesterday while she was sleeping. She had tears in her eyes. The pillow was soaked.

Allah, please guide me in a good way, I want you to give all the happiness to my daughter, if something is evil please take it away from her, I am ready to give everything for my children, please take care of them.

She sleeps worrying about her daughter's future.

✷✷✷

The whole day was so tiring for Lumra and when she comes home, she doesn't have any idea about the cancellation of that proposal. As usual, she did all her work at home, then she overhears her mother's conversation. She knows that it is related to her marriage, even though she doesn't like to overhear someone's talk, for the first time she did that.

Yesterday your sister-in-law asked me about that

As You Wish, Mother

proposal, I told her that the proposal is now broken and she felt pity and I told her who knows Allah's plan. Let's see.

She doesn't want to hear more, all that she wants she heard from her mother's mouth. She is very happy now. She wants to jump and wants to tell everyone that she is very happy. She thanks Allah for helping her. The conversation is going on but she doesn't want to show her mother that she is overhearing her conversation, so she goes into her room. After some time she goes to her mother and asks what to cook. Zainab doesn't reply properly. She knows that her mother is still angry with her, but she is going to be patient, now the proposal is broken, so she can somehow manage her mother to speak with her.

✲✲✲

After so many days, today Lumra sleeps in peace.

"After so many days I am seeing you happy. What happened?" Asks Shafiya.

"Do you know, that proposal has been broken," Says Lumra with a grin.

"How? Why?"

"I don't know how and why it happened. I just overheard my parents talking."

"So, now you are happy. Right?"

"Yes, I am."

"Nice. What is this? Are you reading something?"

"This is a novel. I am going to write a novel, so I just want to know how others are writing. I am reading different novels which are known for their unique techniques so that I can write a good novel. To write a novel I should have vast knowledge so, I have planned to read as many novels as I can. Even though I have read many novels before, now I am going to look deep into it."

"So, I am a friend of an author."

"Author" the mere word makes Lumra's heart burst with happiness. She is not able to describe that emotion. Her mind starts to think about her future, and her interviews on paper and television. Like her favourite authors, she too will get awards for her

As You Wish, Mother

works, she will visit her fans and people will wait to get her autograph. She can become an inspiration to people.

"Not now. But soon will be." Lumra winked.

"Lumra clean the house properly?"

"Why mom?"

"Look at the house, it is very untidy, that's why. If someone visits us uninformed, they will think that this is a bachelor's house. They won't believe an educated young girl lives here. Clean it properly."

Why people should come to my home I am not interested, you are all bringing only headaches. She thought.

"Yes, mom."

Lumra cleans her home with fear and wishes that no one comes to her home because she wants a peaceful day, not another rough day.

13

"I believe she overheard our conservation, Manzoor."

"Right. Look at her, she's just like before. Happy. Bubbly."

"Hmm. At least she is happy. Let us pretend that we don't know that she knows. Her happiness is my priority. Her smile lights up our world."

"Yes, dear. And what about the Mehaboob family marriage?"

"I think we should take our children to the wedding because we don't have any elders in our home to take care of our children. Leaving them alone is not at all safe because we can't trust anyone these days."

"Then I'll book a ticket for everyone and let it be a surprise for them."

"That would be great."

***

Lumra keeps her bag on the table. Her classmates were talking and she sits in her usual place.

Why are you crying? Don't worry it's just your mother no one else.

Lumra listens to the faded voices. She usually doesn't get intimidated by others' conversations, but today she goes to ask what happened.

"Hi, Girls. I know that I am interfering in your conversation. Can you tell me what happened? Is everything alright?"

"No, it's not like that Lumra, her mother scolded her. That's why."

"Why? What happened?"

"Whichever proposal comes for her, she gets rejected because she is overweight. If not rejected then they ask for a huge sum of dowry. That's why her mother scolded her."

As You Wish, Mother

She sees her classmate crying.

"I don't know Lumra, why my parents are like this. When I was young I was thin so they used to insist me to eat but now, they scold me for I am fat. What I did do to suffer like this? They know that the one who is fat and ugly will not get any proposals, then why did they give food? Why didn't they let me starve at a young age? They want a fluffy baby, not a fat daughter. Now they are accusing me of my body. Why this society is like this? Can't he marry the one who is fat? What if I tell them that I will not marry the one who is fat? We don't have the right to tell that. We should marry the person whom our parents choose for us, we should not think about his age, color, or weight. Even if he is double our age we should marry, even he is obese we should marry him and even if he is dark we should marry him. But, if he feels I am older, dark, or massive, he can very well reject me. Or else he will ask dowry to marry me. Am I a product who is brought up just to sell in a market?" She continues to sob.

Lumra can relate her feeling to her as they both are somewhere or the other in a similar situation. Lumra hugs and consoles her, "Don't worry about what your mother said. Even if our parents are good, society will shape their thoughts as per their convenience. You know, we are in the same boat. I just want to be free and become someone respectable in society, but I am suffering because I am born and brought up in a patriarchal society that wants me to get married and give birth to a child before I turn twenty-five."

Amritha Ma'am enters the classroom and interrupts their conversation by greeting the class. She is one of the most vibrant teachers Lumra has ever seen. She always talks about feminism and pinpoints the loopholes in it. Her class is always interactive and enlightening.

"Girls, it's been a long time since we met. I was stuck up with many works. It's already late. This hour is going to end. So I thought of making this lecture interactive. As we all know I teach women's studies. I am going to ask one question. What do you feel about marriage? Why do parents insist their girls to marry soon? What do you think about the dowry system.?"

"Ma'am, I think because parents feel this is the correct age and I feel marriage is important to a girl because she can't live without a man's support. And as we live in a patriarchal society, it is fine to ask for dowry." one girl replied.

Not everyone is satisfied with this response. Few of them frown.

Everyone tells their opinion but Lumra couldn't tell what she thinks. Something in her hinders her feeling. She doesn't express her opinion.

I think Parents just wanna complete their duty as soon as possible. This society treats women as nothing but a toy. A woman is not a human but a product to be sold in the marriage market. The girl just must obey what others are saying and behave like a puppet, nothing more. The boy's side is the consumer and the girl's side is the seller. But the irony here is the seller needs to give the money for taking care of the product.

The bell rang.

"I did not get what I was expecting. Think deeply about it and come up with your opinions. We will discuss it in the next lecture."

***

"Mom, I am home." Says Lumra, while she enters the hall.

"Lumra, pack your things." Said Zainab.

As You Wish, Mother

"Why Mom?" She is confused.

"You two are also coming with us", but this doesn't make Lumra much happy, one reason she already guessed, another is she is afraid of marriage proposals. She hates such occasions. She starts to pack her luggage and informs about this to Shafiya and asks her to note down everything that happens in class.

Zainab's family is now in Chennai to attend the marriage. Lumra also tries to enjoy the marriage function. Lumra helps the bride and she speaks with everyone. When someone talks about her marriage she feels irritated. She is with her mother waiting to enter the dining hall. Suddenly, an old lady comes in front of her and asks her mother, "What is your daughter doing?"

"She is studying B.A. (English)." Replies Zainab.

"Why do you allow her to study? Get her hitched with a nice boy, soon. Teach her cooking. B.A. English won't help her, but round chapattis surely will. Also, she won't be working after her studies, so why are you wasting your hard-earned money on her studies? Use this money in her wedding." The lady doesn't wait for the response and walks away.

Did we ask you anything? From where you are all coming? Just now I escaped from these problems and now you are starting it again. Why can't you people leave me? You are changing my mother's mood always. GROSS.

Lumra is standing in one corner of the wedding hall looking at something and she feels someone's hand on her. She turned that side. Mehboob is standing there. Lumra congratulates her.

"Lumra, can I speak with you for a minute?

Lumra senses that something is again going to happen. But she couldn't deny it. So she follows her. They sit in a secluded place in the marriage hall. Mehboob clears her throat and asks, "Do you know how the proposal broke?"

"I don't know, aunt." *And I don't want to get reminded about that too, please leave me, and don't remind that to me.*

"I know you are not interested in that, but I want you to know that your mother and I were talking yesterday night, she told me that those people accused you of having an affair with someone. And that's the reason your parents want you to get married soon. After hearing this, your mother burst out on those people and came back."

Lumra's heart breaks into tiny pieces.
"How could they judge me? Do they know me? If I am not interested in getting married then that doesn't mean I have an affair. The fault is in their thinking. NARROW MIND. Huh." All these thoughts occupied her mind.

"Lumra..." Mehboob pokes her which brings back Lumra to reality. "Your mom is not young anymore, she already has some medical problems. She is still working, because she just wants to make you all happy, but you are not supporting her. Do you believe your mom?"

"Yes, I do believe her." Lumra saves the tears in her eyes.

"Then don't cry if someone comes to visit you. Just believe your mom. Tell her that you believe her, and assure her that you are happy with her decision. You are an understanding child. Please accept the proposal, your mom will think about all the factors then only she will consider the proposal. So, try to be mature in your thoughts." Mehboob pats her back and leaves.

Lumra starts to cry but makes sure that no one is watching her. She covers her mouth with her hands and cries without letting out any noise.

Why Allah, why am I always stuck in this situation? I don't want to be a burden on my mom. Look, how much I hurt her now? I hate myself. I don't want to hurt her anymore. Allah, please be with me. Please show me the path. Just give me the strength to accept whatever comes my way.
She cries continuously. Am I thinking wrong? I just want to make my family proud, I want to write a book, I want to explore the places, and I want to be a part of literature which I love more than my life, is this wrong? I can't handle this anymore. She wipes her tears and joins her parents. She tries to be away from Mehboob. She knows that the days in Chennai are going to be tough for her.

✳✳✳

"At marriage, many people come to me asking about our daughter, even some rich people came, but I didn't give much attention to them." Says Zainab.

Lumra is half asleep and she listens to her mother's conversation.

"Even some approached me, but we can't decide anything soon. Let her first finish her studies." This made Lumra's day special. She is very happy with her father's words. She pretends to sleep for a while.

✲✲✲

Lumra. It is morning. Wake up!

"Yes, mom."

She then prepares herself for the seminar, that she is going to take on that day.

14

Lumra is in her class writing something in her note. Suddenly, Priya Ma'am enters the classroom; everyone greeted her. Priya Ma'am is known for her perfection.

"Girls, we have our Jubilee this month for that I want students for montage and singing. Interested students, raise your hands."

As usual, nobody raised their hands. Lumra raises her hands, for the sole purpose to be away from her house and she wants to crack her stage fear. She asks Shafiya to join with her, but, she said that her parents will not like this. Lumra then tries to convince Grace, she pretends as if she is not aware of anything, but Lumra succeeds. Finally, Grace also joins her. Ms. Priya jotted down their names and went to the next Classroom.

Lumra then informs her parents and tells them that she

will be late home for a few days. In singing, she meets two important people.

Lumra is in the classroom where choir people were sitting. She sees two girls in front of her chatting continuously and laughing. She is just curious to talk to them, but she doesn't know how to start the conversation. So, she kept mum. She, as usual, starts her conversation with Grace. But something in her eagerly waits to talk with them.

Ziya is very active and she lives in the moment. She is curious about everything that surrounds her, she just loves nature and sings well, she is very obedient to her parents and has only one daughter to her parents, so, she is the gem of the family. Lumra thinks of her as a sister, she loves her innocence and she feels like Ziya reminds her of something which she forgot long back. The other one is Mary Williams, she is a jovial girl but she has her insecurities like Lumra, she gives her love and cares about every single person. She loves to help people, she is innocent and caring, she never hurts anyone and she gives her best in everything but she has some fears just like Lumra.

Lumra spends most of her time with choir people in college, she loves to be with them, and she feels happy and contented when she is surrounded by them, she just starts to love the world, the way she did before.

***

"Lumra get ready. We are going to visit your uncle's home." Informs her mother.

Lumra feels something is wrong. Because one day she went to her aunt's place where the groom's people were waiting for her. So, she feels this day is going to be the same as that day. She just hates it so she wears a very normal dress without her parent's will and goes to her uncle's place.

In the beginning, she doesn't feel comfortable, but gradually she feels good. However, she is conscious as there are more people. Unfortunately, she didn't wear any good dress, so she gets scolded by her mother often. But, Zainab doesn't have any idea about what rattles in her daughter's mind. They finish their lunch and they enter a room.

"Can't you wear any good dress? Look at them, how beautifully dressed they are. Aren't they? I doubt whether you are normal or not. Why you are not at all concentrating on your appearance? What should I do to you, Lumra? Huh." Zainab yelled at her.

Lumra realizes how much she has changed. She couldn't believe that she is living full of confusion and insecurities now. She is living with fear, she is worried all the time, and she is away from her house all the time. She scrutinizes herself, she lives like a puppet, without any lively emotions. She is only filled with anxiety about her future and filled with terror in her mind and soul. She is now afraid that how she is going to continue her life like this. She realizes that once she was always excited to come out and explore the world and loved to visit new places, but now she is running away her old enthusiasm died ages ago, and now she is filled with self-doubts, fear, and melancholy.

✳✳✳

"Don't you feel our daughter is away from us?" Zainab asks Manzoor. She feels something wrong with Lumra'sbehavior but she doesn't have any idea about it.

"Why do you feel like that?"

"She is not at all staying at the home these days and I

think she pretends that she is happy but I can feel that she is not well, I am not able to understand what is spinning around her mind. I just want our daughter to be happy that's it."

"Zainab, you must be overthinking. Our daughter is perfectly alright, she is participating in many programs and that's the reason she's not home most of the time. Also, she is in her final year. She will be free when her studies are over. Don't spoil your mind thinking about anything. Now go to sleep."
Manzoor advises her. But Zainab, a concerned mother she is, is not at all convinced.

The strongest relationship in the world is between a mother and child. A mother can read her child's mind by looking at her. They both live for each other but fail to understand each other's feelings. This Relation always demands sacrifice, a mother should sacrifice her dream for her daughter or vice versa.
Alas! It's always a woman who is expected to sacrifice.

15

"When are they planning to come?" Zainab asks Manzoor.

"They will be here on Sunday."

Lumra overhears their conversation.

Why Allah? Why this happens to me, can't I be happy for some time? I don't have the strength anymore. Let it happen. I just don't want to hurt my parents. Give me enough strength to tackle this problem. I should face this and I know that you will help me to go through this. I just want to become an author, that's it. For that, I can't hurt them.

Around 5 pm, she wakes up. She took a pretty long afternoon nap today. Her eyes are wet, so she wipes them and enters the kitchen, does her usual work and at the same time, she tries her best to behave normally. Whenever she is about to cry, she runs to the bathroom.

"Mom, what to cook for dinner?"

"Whatever you wish to cook. On Sunday some of your father's friends are coming to our home. So, clean home properly. Ok?" Lumra nods with a make-believe smile on her face for she knows why they are coming. This time she is going to behave well, she tries to hide all her emotions by wearing a smiling mask and going to her room.

Why is this so hard for me? Do I have any problems? Everyone gets excited when it comes to marriage and is very eager to get married, but why am I not? I know, my mom will always think about my future then why am I resisting her thoughts on this matter? Don't I fancy marriage? I don't know whether I am wrong or right.

Her eyes produce heat with her emotions and tears finding their way through her cheeks, she wipes out her tears and comes out from her room, normally. Her mother knows everything but now she fails to understand her daughter's feeling.

"When are your friends coming home?" Zainab asks Manzoor in the dining hall.

"They will be here by six o'clock on Sunday." And he turns his head and tells Lumra, "Wear good clothes when they visit us. They are so important to me, do you remember one uncle whom we once met at the hotel, he is coming."

"Yes, Dad." Says Lumra but Zainab senses the hesitation in her voice. Suhail eats his dinner happily and goes to sleep.

While Lumra was washing the dishes, Zainab sees her sobbing.

"Lumra, why are you crying?" Zainab asks.

"No, Amma. I am fine."

"I know you. Don't fool me. Your father told me not to tell you about the proposals, but I think you should know about them. On Sunday they are coming to visit you, listen, I am not at all interested in any of your drama, now. I have already got hurt many times and I am done with it. This is your father's plan, if you want to make him feel ashamed in front of his friends, I don't care. You better behave yourself, Lumra. Stop acting as if we are torturing you or abusing you."

As You Wish, Mother

She tells everything to her daughter. But this time, she's strict.

Lumra's nose gets red because of her constant crying. She is not even sure why she is crying. What is she up to? Is she a perfect daughter to her mother or not? Along with her eyes, her throat too gets parched. She drinks a glass of water and washes her face. She goes to the bathroom and looks at herself in a mirror. Her eyes are no happier but they are swollen with sadness.

She tries to write her feelings down in her diary. She couldn't tell Pinky because she is too weak to do so. Her hand shivers while writing. Half-heartedly, she keeps Pinky in the drawer and goes to sleep.

On jubilee's day, Lumra doesn't want to spoil her mood, so she informs her mother that she will be in college the whole day, even though there is no need for her. She just wants to enjoy her day. Today she is going to face numerous people, she never climbs on stage, because, she is too afraid to face people. This time she broke all her fears and for the first time, she is going to sing and act on stage. She wants to forget about her home and her problems. She just wants to enjoy her day. She has many things to enjoy, especially she has Ziya and Mary Williams to make her forget all her problems, and they are her stress busters. She feels like they are her sisters.

"Hello Ma'am", Lumra enters into the class where the entire choir is preparing something.

They are making a flower bouquet for the choir. She too joins them, somehow she spoke with Ziya and Mary a few days back which made her feel close to them now.

"Akka, ma'am wants to see you," Ziya tells Lumra. For the first time, she is speaking to her.

"Oh...Ok. Coming. Do you know why she is calling me?" Lumra asks Ziya. She tells Grace that she will be there in a moment and goes with Ziya.

"No Akka, I don't know. Akka what is your name?"

"My name is Lumra. You are Ziya, right?"

"Yes, Akka! How do you know my name?"

"It's very simple because your name is popular here."

Ziya blushes a little and says, "No Akka, you are popular."

"Don't joke," Lumra smirks.

"I mean it Akka. Look even now ma'am wants you. Now tell me who is popular?"

"Fine. We both are popular." They both laugh. "Where is ma'am?"

"She is near the English department." Ziya goes to finish her work.

Lumra talks to her professor and then go back to class. "Hi Akka! What did ma'am say?"

"Nothing serious. Just about my answer sheet. That's it. Why are you sitting here alone?"

"Mary Akka just now went to fetch some water so, I am waiting for her. Hey look, here she comes".

Ziya introduces both of them.

"Hi, Akka!"

"Hi, Ziya! Hi Mary!"

"Girls any two of you come here." Says Celina Ma'am.

Mary and Lumra quickly go to Celina Ma'am. She asks them to look into a decoration for a while.

Ziya is with other mates while Lumra is working with Mary.

"Akka what sort of music do you like?" Mary asks Lumra.

"Mmm…Any sort especially melodies and pop music. What about you?"

"Even I like Pop and Melody. Which language, Akka?"

"Tamil and sometimes English. After I chose English as my major, only then I started to listen to English music. What about you?"

"I am mostly into English songs.."

"What will you do next after your UG degree, Akka?"

"I don't know, if my parents allow me, I want to do PG. In sha Allah."

"What is In sha Allah akka?"

"In sha Allah means if God wills."

" oh... ok Akka. You will do further studies Akka. In sha Allah. Surprisingly, your parents are letting you study. Because some of my friends got married after they finished their 12th grade. I think your mother loves you a lot".

"Yes, they do love me a lot which sometimes is a barrier."

"I didn't get you!"

"Leave it. You tell me what will you do after your studies. You have one more year left."

"I am going to do my higher studies in Chennai."

"Will your parents allow you?"

"Akka I am from Chennai and even if I want to go to any other place they will let me."

Wow! Great my parents never leave me to any places.

"What you want to be, Akka, and what is your dream?"

"My dream is to become an Author. And I want to help people out there, especially women who are all suffering because they are not able to or are not allowed to fulfill their dreams. I want to enlighten their life. The most painful thing in life is not getting or achieving your dream. At the worse not getting a chance to let it out. No one is afraid of failure, they are afraid of not getting a chance. In this society, a girl can't say that she wants to live her life. Here, women the term itself is a synonym for Sacrifice. I don't know why!"

"Akka, even I think the same. Akka do you like feminism? I mean are you ok with tagging yourself as a feminist? Because many were afraid to mention themselves as a feminist."

"I feel like it is not something to be afraid of, it is an ideology. Each one has its own take on it. What do you think?"

"Even I feel the same Akka. What does feminism mean to you?"

"I feel feminism is an emotion. For me, it's more than a term. I question every day when will that day comes when we will get to do things without a barrier. And I am unanswerable to my own question. We live in a society where a girl isn't allowed to do things and live the way she wants to because all she is forced to think is about society. A woman is capable of lot many things and not just limited to taking care of the family, however, the stereotypical mindset of our surroundings never understands this. Girls in most cases are not able to achieve their dreams because the societal barrier comes in the way. And even after compromising everything, in the end, it's always her who gets hurt.

And I have a lot to say but not today, some other day, for sure."

"Akka super Akka."

After some time Grace too enters the room. They start their rehearsals, they nearly practiced 3 hours continuously and ma'am permits them to go home but Lumra stays there itself. For now, the whole day is reserved for her only, she starts to enjoy her day, and she wants to enjoy the day as if she has no other day in her life.

Akka Hide and seek in the department it will be fun!!!
Akka can we watch a movie I am feeling bored!!!!
Akka I am feeling hungry....what about you.... what do you bring for lunch?......can we buy something from the canteen......
What sort of books do you read? Akka which actor do you like?.... You know my mom says I was a naughty child when I was young........You know I never knew I could sing on stage.........Akka do you like to watch cartoons?.....

They talked about many things. She feels very happy with them. The whole afternoon was filled with happiness for her

As You Wish, Mother

The program is going to start in the evening, so, everyone starts to come to college. Lumra changes her clothes and she is in charge of the hairdo, so, she accompanies the other two girls and starts to help others. It was fun, because, sometimes she couldn't do it properly, and sometimes it gets messier, but at last the output is good. Ma'am orders them to gather backstage. Everyone goes there. Lumra is with Grace, Ziya, and Mary. They talked about many things. Lumra talks about how she has improved in these three years of graduation.

"What about you, Ziya?" Lumra asked her.

"I don't have anything special, I want to become a singer and I am going to get married after I finish my postgraduate, my parents too wish the same and I am happy about it and I am also eager to lead a beautiful life."

Lumra never talked about her marriage openly, because she feels if she starts to talk about her marriage her parents will think that she is ready for the marriage. It is quite strange for Lumra to listen to Ziya's thoughts on marriage. She talks about it without any hesitation. The program starts and everyone enters the green room.

Now it is Lumra's program time, they go on stage, and Lumra sees a huge crowd in front of her, and she is reminded of how once she blabbered in front of many people in her school days. But, now she gained strength, she starts to sing with her choir. Her heart started to beat faster, but she now dares to overthrow her fears.

They did a good job everyone complimented them. Lumra is proud of herself. But when she realizes that she is going home, she feels pressure in her heart. For a moment she wants to freeze this moment, where she finds her whole happiness.

Ma'am hugs everyone and Lumra comes out from the green room. Grace and others are stuck up with some work. She sees Shafiya outside of the auditorium. Shafiya was absent for three days, she doesn't know why, so, she goes near her.

"Hi, Shafiya how was our program? Did I perform well?" Lumra asked.

"You sang well and acted very well." Says Shafiya enthusiastically. Lumra finds Shafiya's hands filled with *Mehendi*.

"Why did you put *Mehendi*? Did you go for any marriage? And why are you absent for the past three days?" Lumra asks her.

"Nothing." Says Shafiya, but Lumra feels that is not true so she asks her another time.

"I am engaged to my uncle's son." Says Shafiya.

Lumra was shocked. She knows that she is going to marry him one day or the other because Shafiya herself admitted that her father wants her to marry her uncle's son. But, she didn't know that she will get engaged so early.

"Why? What happened suddenly?"

"Nothing much. My father wants me to get engaged to him soon and I just want them to be happy so… I am also happy with it. I know whatever they do that is for my good." Shafiya says normally. But *this is the thing that never comes out of Lumra's mouth.*

Shafiya's mother comes and takes Shafiya home. Lumra wishes her. Lumra is waiting for her father's

As You Wish, Mother

arrival. She is confused. How others don't have a problem with marriage and only she has a problem.

Shafiya and Ziya are happy with their parent's decision. But why can't she? She never fell in love with someone? Why she feels insecure about marriage, she doesn't know. She has many doubts about her, she thinks that she has some mental illness, and she just wants to go to counseling.

Lumra's father arrives and she goes with him. She is very quiet. She tells everyone that she is very tired and wants to sleep early. She tries to sleep, but she couldn't. She feels she is nothing but a lump of clay that has no significance on its own, it will change according to the person's will.

16

"Lumra, are you ready?" Asks her mother.

Lumra wipes out all her tears and comes out from her room. "Here, Ma." Says Lumra. Zainab makes her wear jewelry. She was standing still without speaking anything. *Allah, please help me I don't want to cry in front of people. I want to stay strong. I know you will be here with me.*

The boy's family will be at her place at any minute. Lumra as always stays in her room. Lumra is sitting there alone. She hears the voices coming from outside. They are giggling and chatting about something, probably about the boy. She sometimes hears her parent's voices and the strong voice of men and other voices. She is sitting there, numb.
Some people enter her room. A young lady asks her to stand next to her so that she could measure her height, to compare with the boy. She probably is the groom's sister.

As You Wish, Mother

"What is your name?" Asks an elder woman.

"I am Lumra." Says Lumra.

"What are you studying?" Asks the young lady.

"I am an English literature student."

"What?"

"B.A. English."

"Oh, ok. I am the boy's sister. She is his mother", and she introduces everyone in that room and Zainab asks some questions to them. After some more talking, they leave the house. Zainab was ready to shout at that moment.

"Why didn't you smile at them?" Zainab asked her.

"Ma, I did smile at them, I never cried in front of them." Says Lumra very weakly, because she already has lost all her strength.

Mom why can't you see that I am trying. Mom, I can't

As You Wish, Mother

hold this. It's hurting a lot. Just console me. I am not the same. I want your love mom.

"Lumra, I don't know when you are going to change. You are not a child anymore it is our duty to get you to marry. I am fed up with you."

Lumra doesn't know what is the problem with her, as well as Zainab doesn't know what is the problem with her daughter. She feels insecure as a mother. Because she doesn't know what is going on in her child's mind. She wants to see her daughter smile the way she used to. She is ready to do anything for her happiness and at the same time, she also wants to make sure that she has a beautiful future, for that she is ready to go against her will.

Lumra leaves for college.

While cleaning Lumra's room, Zainab's gaze caught Pinky.
She opens the diary and reads every page. Zainab reads everything; about the conference day, the marriage proposal, how she is fed up with the word 'marriage', her sufferings, her pain, her parent's pain, etc.

Poor Lumra is unaware that Pinky is been read by her mother. She is happy to meet Vinaya.

"Hi, writer, what happened? Why are you looking sad? Is that about any proposal?" Vinaya asks her.

Lumra nods her head, she tries to wipe out her tears without her knowledge. But, Vinaya understands it and brushes her hair and asks her what happen. In the beginning, she hesitates but then she starts to sob and to talk to her.

Zainab flips another page and reads, *Pinky I never want to hurt my mother, I just want to make sure she is happy. I am ready to do anything to make her happy. But I can't do this. I don't know why. I don't know whether is it insecurity or I am afraid of this commitment. I just don't want it now. I have many things to do before my marriage. I don't know what to do please help me.*

"Vinaya, even though I am not at all interested in this I am trying my best, even on that day also I felt suffocated, but I smiled in front of them for the sake of my mother. I want her to be happy. But she didn't recognize it at all."

"Lumra think about your mother, she will always think about her daughter's future, for her, your happiness is more important than anything. I am not saying to go and get married now. It's not that, you need to support her and assure her that you believe her, she feels insecure the same way you do. That's it. Do you think it's only happening to you? You should be happy that your mother is talking to you about all these things. I have some friends who got married soon, even without their will. But your mom fights for you and you are doing your UG degree, you should be proud of this. I know your mom will never stop your studies for marriage."

"I know about all this, but I don't know why I can't make my mind."

Pinky, I just want to speak to my mom, but I am not able to do that, whenever I speak with her, I am unable to see her eyes, because, I couldn't see her eyes filled with sadness and then knowing that I am the reason behind her sadness, it hurts me more than anything. So, today I recorded my feelings on my phone. Because I felt if I keep this to myself, I will blast.

Zainab looks here and there and unfortunately, Lumra has forgotten her phone at home today. She checks her phone and finds a folder name 'MOM'. She opens it and starts to listen.

"Mom, I am Lumra."

She can feel the pain in her voice when she started to speak.

"Vinaya, I don't know what to do? I want to live my life. I am under the care of my parents till this moment. If I get married I will be put into another cage, that's it. I can't bear this anymore and I am not interested in this commitment for now. I am afraid that if I get married now, I will destroy my life. Like other girls, I too have dreams but now that is secondary for me, I want to create my own identity then only I want to think about marriage. I am suffocated by four walls. I just want to spread my wings and fly higher where no one can touch me. I want to live in this world, Vinaya. I desperately want to live. I know my mom sacrificed her life for us. I don't want to regret it later, this is the only life I have, and I don't want to lose it and find happiness somewhere. I want to make this life beautiful for me as well as for my parents. Why is always a girl child ceased from all her emotions? Why can't a girl child fulfill her parent's dream? Why can't a girl dream of building a palace for her parents than just giving them the grandparent's title? I am filled with these questions, Vinaya. I don't have an answer now. But I want to be the answer to these questions."

Mom, I want to hug you and want to tell you that I am bruised and I want your love and care as medicine. I don't know why I hate marriage, whenever I want to talk about this, I am unable to express it... I tried my best to control my feelings and I did, but you failed to recognize that. Many times I thought of committing suicide, because, I know I am the reason for the pain which you are undergoing. I want to be your happiness, not sadness. Many times I didn't talk to you because I am becoming a burden to you....(sobs).... Whenever I realize that you are crying because of me, I feel broken. I lost all my happiness a long time back, mom, I know that I am not the same as I was in my past. I started doubting everything. If you are going outside, even it is for some other purpose I start to think that you are going to talk about my marriage, in my own home I live like an alien, I feel alone all the time. Whenever I cry I am longing for a shoulder to lean on, I want someone to tell me that I am with you and everything will be alright, but I have the only darkroom where the loneliness accompanies me. I feel like dying, mom. To overcome that feeling, I am praying a lot. I stopped praying for the proposal to break. I am praying to Allah that whatever comes my way, I should take the right decision. I know all your prayers and hard work are for us, I know you will choose the best for me but in this marriage thing alone I am not able to say, "AS YOU WISH, MOTHER". I don't know why Mom, I asked this question a million times myself, but I didn't get an answer for it. (Sobs)

"You know I love my home more than anything in the world, but now I am running away from there. All I am doing is, I am searching for different reasons to stay away from my home. I love to be away from home now. I was a different person then, I am a different person now."

Mom, I forgot to smile long back. Now I am smiling just for the sake of you and father. I don't want to hurt you anymore. You lost most of your life thinking about us. I want to give you happiness. It is my turn, mom, I feel happiness does not only rely on marriage. I want to show you the world which you missed at a young age and I want to prove to the world that you both are great parents. I started to act continuously, I am afraid that in these actions, I will lose myself. I want to be normal, Mom. All I remember is sour eyes and sleepless nights, nothing more. I want to sleep, mom. (Her voice breaks) I want to sleep and that too tight sleep without any fear,

I am hungry for the past few days because I couldn't swallow food happily but, you were not there to ask me, whether I eat or not. You have my dad to share your emotions but I don't have anyone. I can't share this with Suhail, he is young and he won't understand this. My friends, I don't know whether they will understand or not, I am afraid that they will think of me as if I am mad. I am becoming insane, mom. Thinking about all this stuff...

Zainab couldn't control her tears. She sits on Lumra's bed and cries.

"One day, I told my mother that I am not feeling well, I don't know in which mood she was but she told me that I am faking weakness purposely. I used to think that if I don't feel well then they will pause this marriage topic for a while.
But all in vain. Since that day, I stopped telling mom about my weak health, even when it's real."

"Are you mad? She would have been in some trouble that is why she told you like that. Why are you harming yourself?"

"It's not self-harming. I just don't know how to control my feelings. I am afraid that I will become mad if I keep them to myself. I have already showered a lot of trouble on them. You know, I feel it's better to die."

"If you talk like this another time I will surely kill you. Do you believe your mother?"

"I believe her more than anyone in the world."

"Do you believe in god?"

"Yes, I know Allah is always there for me."

"Then listen to me. Just forget all about this, just concentrate on your studies, you have a semester coming next month. This is our final semester so give your hundred percent. ok?"

"Yes, I will. I want to prove to my mom, who I am, and I will use this exam for that. Thank you so much, Vinaya. I will be bold and try to tackle my problems, bravely. Let's see who wins this game; so-called social norms or a desperate daughter's dream for her parents."

"That's my girl. Now go and study. All the best."

Lumra hugs Vinaya.

Mom, I can't bear this anymore, I'll try my best hereafter, let Allah decide my life. But, I will fight for my dreams till the end. I can't hurt you anymore. If someone comes, let them come. I will try my best. I won't let you down in any situation. But understand one thing, I am not happy with this thing, I trust you, and I believe you. Mom, I just wanna tell you that I LOVE YOU. I love you as always. It will not change at any cause. I know I have hurt you many times. Please forgive me. Please don't hate me and don't stop talking to me. I don't have anyone except you and our family.

The recording ends. In the whole recording, all Zainab could hear was her daughter's painful sob and her heavy voice. Pinky is now drenched in Zainab's tears.

17

Zainab's heartaches after hearing her daughter's confession, she knows that her daughter is not well, but she never in her wildest dream guessed that her daughter thought of committing suicide. Everything she did until this moment is all for the good of her children. But she never imagined she could be the reason for her daughter's suffering.

"I know she is hurt, but this world is not safe for her. Who will take care of her after my death? I want to make sure that she is in safe hands then only I can close my eyes peacefully. But what can I do now? Allah, please help me! I am ready to take all the suffering from her. I want my child to be happy all the time. I want her smiling face back. I want her to sleep well and eat well. How much she underwent, and how much could that little heart suffer? What should I do now? Until now I believed that she lost her trust in me, but now I have realized that she tolerates all this only to make me happy. My daughter is with me all these times. I am the one who didn't understand her. Why was she born to me, if she had been born into a rich family she would have had all things, they would have helped her to achieve all her dreams, here I am not able to do anything for my daughter."

Grieving Zainab goes into deep thought, she calls someone and hangs up the phone later. She places the note and mobile in the same place and does all the household chores and is eagerly waiting for Lumra to return home.

✳✳✳

After speaking with Vinaya, Lumra goes into deep thought and contemplates within herself.

Am I a good daughter? Did I ever give happiness to my mother? Why am I always struggling to tell her that I believe her and her decisions for me are always right? What can I do to take away all her pain?

Lumra decides something in her mind and then starts to read. She is waiting to go home. She wants to talk to her mother, she is now willing to tell her mother everything.

Ms. Selvi enters the class. She looks very serious. Everyone greets her and she tells the students to sit down.

"Girls, you all know the college givesawards for General proficiency, best outgoing student, and best orator in English to students. So now I want your opinions regarding whom to give these awards to. You know your friends more than I know them. First, suggest me someone for General Proficiency.

Lumra and her classmates shouted, 'Nimmy'.

"Nimmy, get up! So, you have selected Nimmy (Points her then turns to students) for General proficiency. Now for the best outgoing student and for this award, the student should not only be good in studies but also helpful and excel in co-curricular activities. Now tell me?"

Everyone shouted along with Lumra and Shafiya, 'Grace'.

"Grace, stand up! Everyone claps for her. Now Ms. Selvi clears her throat and asks the students, who are you suggesting as the best orator in English? For this, the student's medium of instruction at school should not be Engish. Suggest me the one whom you feel improved a lot in their language and proved herself to you during their college days."

Will a single soul utter my name? Lumra thought to herself. *The miracle happened even before she started thinking.* The whole class suggested her name. She never thought that she had made this much impact on her class. But she has. She feels like she stands high on the mountain and the chill breeze embraces her heart. As usual, her heart beats faster but this time, it is full of happiness.

"Any other name you want to suggest?" Asks Ms. Selvi.

"LUMRAAA…." The voice is still louder. Lumra feels as if she has accomplished everything. This is what she always wanted from her first day of college, acknowledgment. This is what she wants to prove to her mother that she is born to do something great and this is the first step towards it.

"Any more suggestions?"

As You Wish, Mother

"LUUMMRAA....."

Lumra couldn't withhold her happiness, her cheeks start to ache because of her happiness.

"Any other suggestion than Lumra?"

Everyone including Lumra says ' Shafiya'.

"Ok. I thought of these two people that's why I asked you. Lumra you are going to receive an award as the best orator in English."

Lumra stands up and says, "Yes ma'am," her face turned bright pink.

She now just wants to go home and tell her mother that she will obey her mother as well as wants to tell her about her achievement for which she strived hard.

✷✷✷

"After you are done cleaning the dishes, do the dusting of the house."

"Sure. Is someone coming home to visit, mom?"She smiles.

"No one is coming to our home. Do you need someone to come to our home to clean it?"

"No Mom. Just asked."

"When is your exam going to start?"

"Next month, mom."

"When will they issue applications for M.A?"

"By this month-end. Why mom?"

"If your college issues applications, do get one application for you. The proposal got canceled. You continue your study if we get a good proposal, we will get you married to him. Don't stress yourself much and study. Tell me how much the application costs, ok?"

"Yes, mom."

Zainab could sense how happy her daughter is. She brushes her hair and asks her to do her work.

I don't know Lumra, how I canceled that proposal and now I am permitting you to study more. I only care about your happiness. I will do anything and everything for you. You are my happiness. I am not sure whether this will continue or not, but I will assure you that I'll try my best to help you, other than that Allah is there to guide me. For now, be happy, don't think about anything, and sleep well my daughter, your mom loves you always.

Meanwhile, Lumra is surprised.

What happened just now? How did it happen? I thought of telling mom that I will not cry if someone comes here, but, there is a total change. How can it happen? Thanks, Allah.

Lumra serves dinner and Zainab can see the real happiness on her daughter's face.

"Did you eat?" Asks Zainab.

"Yes, mom." Says Lumra She is unaware of what happened today between Pinky and her mother. Even Manzoor doesn't have any idea about it. Zainab doesn't want to disclose the incident to anyone. She decided to bury it within herself.

"Mom I forgot to tell you one thing!"

"What Lumra?"

"Mom, I am going to receive an award for my proficiency in English. This is for the students who are from the different medium of instruction other than English." Without taking a break she tells everything to her parents. Her face is now filled with happiness. Zainab could feel that.

"Good, keep it up and do your best in your PG too." Says Zainab. She feels very proud of her daughter.

For the first time in a long time, everyone goes to sleep light-hearted.

Dear Pinky,

I don't know what happened today. Today is the most tiring day I ever had. Today, I spoke with Vinaya, my friend, about my fear of marriage and I decided to accept what comes in my life. I am going to receive an
award for the first time in my life, then here at my home, things were different. You know what? My mom permitted me to pursue higher education. I am very happy about it, I told Grace, and she too was

very happy about it. Pinky, you know I even finished my novel outline.
I was really afraid that how I am gonna finish my novel in a month. But now I have a solid two years and I will work hard on my novel. And I will try my best to publish it. When I am talking about publication, I am thinking about how wonderful it would be. Who will be my publisher? And will I be called for a book signing? Will I be called for speech? How it will feel I don't know. But I don't want to be anxious about it.

Love you, pinky, and thank you for being with me.

With love,
Lumra.

Lumra doesn't know whether this will last long or not. She knows it may change in a day or two. Or it will cause some other problem afterward, but now she doesn't want to think about any things, she just wants to be happy with what has happened now. She closes her diary and keeps it in her safe place. She tucks herself into bed with a peaceful mind. Today she will have peaceful sleep.

Zainab now closes her door, after confirming that her daughter went to sleep. Now she can also sleep well.

Both mother and daughter go to their dream world in their sleep.

We don't know what will happen to Lumra's dream. I don't know who is the winner here: Mother's love or daughter's love.Overall the love between the mother and daughter wins together.

Let's hope it has a beautiful ending.

I am here to give you this novel in your hands, just shape them the way you want...

The new beginning starts from here.

You can contact the publisher at:
www.fanatixxpublication.com

www.ingramcontent.com/pod-product-compliance
Lightning Source LLC
LaVergne TN
LVHW041944070526
838199LV00051BA/2899